Libraries and Graduate Students

This book gathers together a variety of perspectives and approaches toward building relationships between academic libraries and a unique scholarly population with specific needs—graduate students. This valuable resource shares efforts about specific programs and strategies to enhance and enrich the graduate student experience. Contributions to this volume include a wide variety approaches though case studies, an extensive literature review on academic integrity, an initiative for program development in the context of a broader education initiative, and a chapter on graduate fellowships for manuscripts and special collections.

Many of the approaches integrate tried and true information literacy strategies, but they also put unique 'spins' on these approaches. This book's scope includes large and small colleges and universities, public and private, and specialized and general. Subjects include stand alone courses and workshops, program development, assessment, distance education, online environments, instructional design, and collaborations.

This book is a valuable resource for public service librarians, information literacy/instruction librarians, library science professors, graduate program coordinators, special collections librarians, and subject specialist librarians in all areas.

This book was published as a special issue of *Public Services Quarterly*.

Gretta Siegel is the Science Librarian and Coordinator of Graduate Student Services at Portland State University, in Portland, Oregon.

Libraries and Graduate Students

Building connections

Edited by Gretta Siegel

Routledge
Taylor & Francis Group
LONDON AND NEW YORK

First published 2009 by Routledge
2 Park Square, Milton Park, Abingdon, Oxon, OX14 4RN

Simultaneously published in the USA and Canada
by Routledge
270 Madison Avenue, New York, NY 10016

Routledge is an imprint of the Taylor & Francis Group, an informa business

© 2009 Edited by Gretta Siegel

Typeset in Times by Value Chain, India
Printed and bound in the United States of America on acid-free paper by IBT Global

British Library Cataloguing in Publication Data
A catalogue record for this book is available from the British Library

ISBN 10: 0-7890-3054-3 (h/b)
ISBN 10: 0-7890-3443-3 (p/b)
ISBN 13: 978-0-7890-3054-2 (h/b)
ISBN 13: 978-0-7890-3443-4 (p/b)

CONTENTS

PREFACE

A recurring theme in this volume, and indeed, the reason for this compilation, is that graduate students occupy a unique niche in the academic enterprise–they are more sophisticated in both skills and needs than undergraduates, yet are not quite as adept in navigating the myriad array of resources that their professors are. Thus, it is incumbent upon us to consider approaching information literacy and other forms of engagement with this population in some unique and innovative ways. As teachers, hopeful to impart skills for life-long learning, we need to be examining the graduate environment for developmental opportunities. Another recurring theme in this volume is that there is a dearth of published literature on this topic, and it is hoped that this effort will provide a jumping off point for others to make contributions to this area.

Some of the themes that are addressed, in one or more of the chapters are: distance learning and other remote users, program development, assessment, academic integrity, engagement with collections, credit courses, integrated instruction, and faculty/departmental collaborations. While many of the ideas presented are in the form of 'case studies'–it is hoped that the lessons learned and the ideas discussed will have transferability to a variety of other situations. In addition to being selected for quality, the chapters in this collection were also chosen to provide representation from small, medium, and large schools; from across the disciplines as well as from interdisciplinary approaches; and from both private and public institutions.

Increasingly, many graduate programs, particularly professional programs, are now offered in an online environment. Are these students prepared to conduct serious research? Pival, Lock, and Hunter from the University of Calgary address this question by reporting on an assessment done for students in the field of education. Following this, William Badke from the Associated Canadian Theological Schools, describes the evolution of an information literacy course from a live offering to an online offering, including all of the technical and pedagogical adjustments that had to be made in the process. A third contribution to the 'online learning environment' theme is from Rutgers (the State University of New Jersey), where Sara Harrington investigates how online pathfinders can be better used to target the needs of the graduate population, in this case, in the humanities. As an alternative to either course integration or stand alone credit courses, Jeremy R. Garritano from Purdue University presents a highly effective model for a series of seminars that address the needs of chemistry students in a face-to-face setting.

In the late 1990s, an effort was launched in Europe with the goal of harmonizing the architecture of the higher education system in the EU and launching reforms that would remove barriers to mobility for students and professors by the year 2010.[1] Within this arena, the University of Konstanz in Germany is a leading institution in the information literacy debate. Oliver Kohl-Frey, a librarian deeply involved with this debate, gives a report on how a comprehensive information literacy program can be developed within this context of a much broader initiative.

The next two chapters explore collaborative initiatives within two very different professional programs. The first, from the UCLA Anderson School of Management by Frand, Borah, and Lippincott, describes a highly strategic approach that takes into account the 'student life-cycle' of their graduate students, and presents appropriate 'interventions' at various points in this cycle–with the result being a highly integrated program that promotes sustainable skill development. The second of these chapters is from Western Washington University, where Sylvia G. Tag describes how various assessment exercises resulted in the initiation of a required information literacy course that integrates into the curriculum of a Communication Science and Disorders program.

Academic integrity is an important issue faced by everyone in the university environment, and graduate students receive mixed messages about what really constitutes integrity or dishonesty. An extensive literature review by Patti Schifter Caravello examines this issue in the context of different subject-disciplines, and proposes an instructional and collaborative role for librarians working with graduate students and their teaching faculty. Along similar lines, Judy Xaio and David Traboulay from the College of Staten Island (CUNY) have developed a collaborative course model for liberal arts students that explicitly integrates a strong academic integrity component. This collaboration uses the setting of a master's thesis seminar to holistically integrate information literacy concepts with the extended thesis experience.

In the final contribution, the role of the librarian is more implicit, as the central role of connection building is played by the collections themselves. In exploring the substantial opportunities for humanities graduate students to engage with rare book and manuscript repositories through residential research fellowship programs, Kathryn James posits that engagement with these kinds of fellowship programs performs important developmental functions for young scholars in relevant fields.

Taken together, I believe that this collection demonstrates that the developmental level of graduate students and their studies provides for fertile ground in which to sow the seeds of information literacy skills that can truly take root and grow. Pulling together and editing this collection, and working with the contributors, has been a highly rewarding experience. The enthusiasm with which this proposal was received was very exciting. I would like to thank Jennifer Dorner, of UC Berkeley, for initiating this opportunity. Additionally, I would like to thank the many reviewers who gave their time and extensive comments in reviewing these papers. Special thanks go to Trudi Jacobson, head editor of *Public Services Quarterly* for her keen and patient editorial assistance, and to William Badke, one of the contributors, who graciously provided assistance to many in meeting technical formatting specifications. Finally, I would like to dedicate this volume to two of my mentors–to Joan Ormondroyd, who instilled in me the importance of relevant, integrated bibliographic instruction, and to Maureen Sloan who gave me my first opportunity to really engage with the special niche of graduate student education.

Gretta E. Siegel
Guest Editor

Assessing Research Readiness of Graduate Students in Distance Programs

Paul R. Pival
Jennifer V. Lock
Maureen Hunter

INTRODUCTION

Are students who enter distance graduate programs adequately prepared with the necessary research readiness skills for the new information era? Many professors and librarians would say no, including the authors who have a combined 35 years of academic experience. Graduate students need to have advanced research skills to locate the academic literature that will allow them to meet the expectations of their programs. There is additional pressure on those who are registered in distance programs to enter with these skills or develop them with minimal personal contact. Incoming students who have not conducted research within the past several years may be shocked and overwhelmed at the options available to them through digital library environments and the subsequent difficulties of filtering for the most useful resources.

Immersed in the academic world, professionals have often been hard pressed to adjust to the pace of constant change while graduate students must adjust to a new mode of operation at the same time as learning to identify and locate relevant information without much familiarity with the academic milieu. While it is assumed that people accepted into graduate programs have somehow automatically acquired research skills, this often proves not to be the case (Zhang, 1998). Knowing what is classified as an academic source and knowing where and how to access such items can lead to frustration for new students. Given oft-demonstrated weakness in using academic sources, professors and librarians ask, "What demonstrated research readiness skills do new graduate students actually have, especially those in distance programs?" Based on what they know or don't know, what needs to occur to help them develop this skill set?

This quandary has led the researchers to investigate how others have handled the apparent disconnect between graduate students' (mis)conceptions about what is entailed in academic research and the reality. In contrast to the intensively surveyed first year undergraduate, almost no information exists on the actual abilities of incoming distance graduate students. There seems to be a disconnect between the beliefs of some graduate students that they understand the research process and the actual complexity of the information world that they encounter.

LITERATURE REVIEW

The search for supporting literature was mainly confined to post-1995 research on the question of the demonstrated research skills of graduate students, particularly those in distance programs. The date limit was chosen because earlier material preceded Web-based sources and technologies. In addition, the researchers hoped to discover a previously developed tool which would allow them to measure this skill set of graduate students. The researchers discovered a paucity of research on any aspect of graduate students' actual performance and what little there was dealt with skills required by a particular discipline, usually engineering, education, or biology. Nor were the researchers looking for studies on service or instructional preference. Existing research primarily covers needs assessment, particularly in the area of service provision, selection of materials, or user satisfaction; Unwin, Stephens, and Bolton's (1998) 1997 survey of 1000 British distance learning students is one of the largest and most typical of these. Needs assessments were not of great interest because they rarely provide examples of actual performance. In contrast, the skill and confidence level of undergraduates has been measured extensively, as exemplified by Kunkel, Weaver, and Smith (1996) and Mittermayer (2005). The researchers did not locate much relevant material on information literacy instruction for graduate students which might remedy any lack of confidence that might be identified.

In their large needs assessment of distance learning students in the United Kingdom, Unwin, Stephens, and Bolton (1998) quote students who see no need for training: "Don't feel that this should be necessary–was taught to use a library in primary school" and "Only an idiot would not be able to use a library" (p. 61). In contrast to this certainty, Donaldson (2004) noted that while graduate students are expected to be literate and skilled researchers, "many do not have the required skills and knowledge [and] are easily overloaded with data and information" (p. 1). Brown (2000), who alluded to the exploding complexity of the information world in "Growing Up Digital," points out that the Web is a transformative technology which is rapidly changing the research environment (p. 10). Relating this development to the graduate student experience, Gonzalez (2001) commented "the complexity of the knowledge-based global economy with its wealth of information and opportunities has increased graduate students' desire for help. The more decisions they have to make, the more guidance they want" (p. 1624). Zhang (1998) noted that, "a considerable number of graduate students in educational administration lacked library research and Internet search knowledge and skills" (p. 6). Some research has been done on the role anxiety and lack of confidence may play in graduate students' approaches to research and their performance. Van Kampen (2004) dis-

covered that indeed significant anxiety did exist as students began to realize the number of resources which are now available to them in
contrast to even the previous decade. Anxiety erodes confidence.
Onwuegbuzie and Jiao (1996) have published extensively on the question of library anxiety and note that the many manifestations of library
anxiety "have the propensity to debilitate information literacy" (p. 71).
This appears to contrast with the excessive bravado demonstrated by the
students quoted by Bolton, Unwin, and Stephens (1998) above. Can a
more accurate picture be developed? The OCLC College Students Perceptions of Libraries and Information Resources (2006) was not available at the time this project started, nor did it provide a breakdown by
graduate students. However, it would have reinforced a general feeling of
confidence on the students' part 10 years into the Web revolution.
Again, it did not record actual student performance.

    Leverance (1997) surveyed mature graduate students in the early
days of the Web and found a generally positive attitude to information
technology and a growing degree of confidence in using it. However,
this population had on-campus access to dedicated library help and did
not have to cope with distance issues. Franklin and Toifel (1994) compared graduate and undergraduate students on their retention of content
from bibliographic instruction and found that the graduate students did
not retain new knowledge as well as undergraduates, thus reinforcing
professorial suspicions that graduate students are not always the experts
of expectations. More evidence of a frequent disconnect between student and faculty perceptions of student skill level is noted by Zao and
Zheng (2004) who found that, while distance students in their study reported good or excellent information-seeking skills, " most of them experienced difficulty using the Texas A&M University system
sometimes or often" (p. 31). Bodi (2002) dealt with the gap between
what librarians teach and what students seem to know. She contrasted
the expert scholars' research process with that of undergraduates, show-
ing the very wide divide; perhaps it can be assumed that graduate students are in the middle. If this is true, they will demonstrate uncertainty
about search methods and resources and will not be operating on the
scholars' model at all, despite high personal and supervisory expectations. Neely (2006) would have provided useful guidance in our development of a tool which might have elicited more detail on advanced
searching skills but it was not available as our work began, nor did the
researchers have the time or manpower to develop and validate such a
tool. Neely does state 'Although a great number of information instruments have been developed for college-level students, very few of them

are represented in the published literature, and even fewer are based on the ACRL standards' (p. 153).

The literature review yielded no tools which could readily measure research skills and offer insight into the beliefs of graduate students about their abilities until one of the researchers heard Ivanitskaya, Laus, and Casey speak at the Off-Campus Library Services Conference, May 2004. They described the Research Readiness Self/Assessment (RRSA) tool which could assess "how student research attitudes and perceptions correlate to their actual research skills" (p. 167). The RRSA was not developed specifically for graduate students. It was designed to be used with distance and senior undergraduate learners. The RRSA developers made the following statement:

> In distance learning programs this lack of understanding of the research process and dependence on the Internet in isolated situations in which many distance students find themselves can be magnified. Students researching from remote locations may have fewer opportunities for reference consultations, through which they may learn better research skills. In addition, a significant number of distance learners are older than the traditional college age and feel anxiety about asking for reference assistance since they believe they should already know how to conduct research. (Ivanitskaya, Laus, & Casey, 2004, p. 170)

Given the reputation of Central Michigan University as a leader in distance services, the investigators believed that the RRSA would allow them to gather the information they sought. The RRSA had been validated and tested with a significant number of users and the results compiled into a database. The Central Michigan University team was very gracious in allowing the Calgary researchers to adapt and use the tool and assisted in the process.

INSTRUMENT

The Research Readiness Self/Assessment tool was developed by a team of librarians and researchers at Central Michigan University (CMU). Based on input from Off Campus Services librarians and an extensive literature review, an assessment tool consisting of multiple choice questions, skill-based problems, and measures of students' attitudes was developed. Ivanitskaya, Laus, and Casey (2004) identified the following nine skills or attitudes measured by the RRSA:

1. Online research skills. "Ability to use online library catalogue, online library databases (e.g., FirstSearch) and their Boolean operators" (p. 173).
2. Knowledge of information resources. "Ability to identify and use best scholarly resources, knowledge of terminology" (p. 173).
3. Understanding of plagiarism and copyright issues.
4. Attitudes toward Internet research.
5. Evaluation of information. "Ability to evaluate the quality of full-text articles from scholarly journals" (p. 173).
6. Motivation to supplement readings. "Motivation to supplement instructor-assigned readings with additional materials" (p. 173).
7. Frequency of library use.
8. Likelihood of contacting a librarian.
9. Research experience.

Ivanitskaya, Laus, and Casey (2004) addressed the validity of the instrument by examining content validity, "the degree to which RRSA covers all of the competencies essential to research readiness and information literacy" (p. 177) and concurrent criterion-related validity, "by correlating student scores on the assessment with proxy measures of library use and information skills" (p. 177).

In the appendix of Ivanistskaya, O'Boyle, and Casey's (2006) article, the reader will find the list of questions included in the RRSA.

METHODOLOGY

Research Questions

The aim of this descriptive research study was to assess the skill level and research readiness of selected groups of graduate students within the Faculty of Education's Graduate Division of Educational Research and Applied Psychology at the University of Calgary. The following three questions guided the research to assess graduate student knowledge and feelings of confidence in conducting library research:

- What factors impact the research readiness of graduate students?
- What levels of research readiness confidence are demonstrated by students?
- What degree of research readiness is demonstrated by education graduate students?

Population and Sample

The following three groups of students comprised the study's target population: (1) all students currently enrolled in an online educational doctoral program within the Graduate Division of Educational Research (GDER), (2) all GDER students who were accepted into the certificate, diploma, course-based masters or thesis-based graduate programs (e.g., Masters or PhD) for either July or September, 2005; and (3) all students who had enrolled in January, 2006 in the online Applied Psychology masters program. For each of the groups, students received an e-mail explaining the study and inviting them to participate in it. An e-mail reminder was sent to each student approximately two weeks after the original e-mail invitation. A total of 262 students were invited to participate in this study, and 50 actually completed the assessment, for a response rate of 19.1%. It should be noted that the participants' knowledge as graduate students in general was being tested, rather than their specific knowledge of educational materials.

Instrument Modified for this Study

The researchers slightly adapted the Research Readiness Self Assessment (RRSA) for three reasons: (1) to Canadianize questions, (2) to refer students to University of Calgary sources in the automated feedback, and (3) to elicit additional demographic information (e.g., technology use). Between the administration of the survey to the first two groups of students and the third, the survey was modified so that the Likert scale questions now utilized a Continuous Visual Analog Scale (VAS) (e.g., slider scale). The VAS was a 10-point scale, making direct comparison to the 6-point Likert scale impossible. We have aligned the results from the two scales as shown in Figure 1.

The resulting modified survey consisted of 53 questions:

- 8 utilizing a Likert scale or VAS scale (strongly disagree to strongly agree),
- 32 single-answer multiple choice, and
- 13 multiple choices.

Students received an immediate customized response to their answers that confirmed knowledge and identified areas to be enhanced. This feedback was to be used by students as starting points for remedial

FIGURE 1.

Likert	VAS
0	0 – 1.67
1	1.68 – 3.33
2	3.34 – 5.0
3	5.01 – 6.68
4	6.69 – 8.35
5	8.36 – 10

assistance. The students' answers were stored in an anonymous database used as the data set for this study.

DISCUSSION OF THE FINDINGS

Student Demographics

Bocchi, Eastman, and Swift (2004) suggest that the typical distance learner is older than the average traditional student, even in graduate-level programs (p. 247). The researchers found of the 50 participants, the majority of them were between the ages of 31 and 50. It was found that 20% of the participants were between the ages of 18 and 30, 24% were 31 to 40 years of age, 44% were 41 to 50 years old and 12% were 51 years of age or older. Of the participants, 18 of 50 were pursuing an educational doctorate or a doctor of philosophy degree. Thirty-two of the students were pursuing a master's degree.

Library and Research Experience

The researchers also wondered how much recent experience students had with libraries or research in an online environment. In the previous five years, students reported a number of different types of exposure to the library (refer to Table 1).

Table 2 shows that students reported that they used the library on a fairly regular basis in the year prior to their completion of the assessment. Thirty-eight percent of the respondents indicated that they used libraries once per month or less, though another 48% used the library at least once per week. In an additional question, participants were asked to note how frequently they accessed a library Web site. It was found that 42% of them accessed it every day, several times a week or once a

TABLE 1. What library instructional services were you exposed to in the last 5 years? Check all that apply:

Library Services	Number of Responses
A for-credit library class	4
A non-credit library instruction presentation or session	20
Online library help guides or tutorials	33
Printed instructions on library use	18
None of the above	10

TABLE 2. How often did you use libraries during the past year? Include library visits, online access to library resources, contacts with library staff members, etc.

Frequency of Usage	Number of Responses
Every day	1
Several times a week	14
Once a week	9
Every 2 weeks	7
Once a month	10
Less than once a month	9

week. Thirty-four percent access it either every two weeks or once a month.

It is evident from the responses that the participants have been in various levels of contact with library staff in the year preceding the assessment. Thirty-six percent of respondents indicated they have contacted staff six or more times. Forty percent have been in contact between two and five times and the remaining 24% had only one or no contact with staff (refer to Table 3).

Students were asked to identify the types of academic activities they had engaged in during the past year. They were given a list of seven items and they could check more than one response. It was found that 26% of the respondents indicated that they had talked to a library staff member about their research topic. Fifty-two percent indicated that they wrote a summary of the main ideas of an article, book, or other document. Forty-eight percent noted that they had evaluated the quality of literature cited by the author. Fifty percent noted they had found suggestions for additional materials through prefaces, footnotes, or endnotes. Seventy percent had authored a paper that put together ideas from multiple sources. Forty percent had obtained information from the Internet to

Libraries and Graduate Students

TABLE 3. How many contacts with library staff members did you have during the past year? Count the total number of face-to-face, phone, fax, e-mail, or any other types of contacts:

Number of Contacts	Number of Responses
10+ contacts	11
6-9 contacts	7
4-5 contacts	5
2-3 contacts	15
1 contact	6
None	6

make a health-related decision. Fourteen percent had not engaged in any of the above-mentioned activities within the past year.

Seventy-eight percent of students indicated that subject headings or other controlled vocabulary would be the technique they would use to research academic topics. In contrast, 38% noted that scholarly encyclopedias or dictionaries would be useful in researching academic topics and 78% would use indexes to journal, magazine or newspaper articles as an approach.

Overall, the students who participated in this survey appear to be fairly well versed with libraries and claim a fair amount of research experience.

Student Perception of Research Readiness

With the RRSA online assessment, several questions were designed to create a profile of student perceptions of their library and Web-based research skills. A clear majority of students rated their overall research skills as being good, very good, or excellent. Less than one third of the students rated their skill level to be fair or poor (refer to Table 4).

A second question asked them to rate their skill at conducting library research at the graduate level. Table 5 shows that students were not quite as confident in this area with responses ranging from very poor to very good. However, a large majority of the students rated their confidence as being between fair to very good.

Table 6 illustrates that most students felt quite confident in their skill of judging the quality of information from print or electronic sources. Three of the 50 respondents rated their ability as being excellent.

For finding high quality information in narrow topics, students were more evenly distributed in their self-assessment. As noted in Table 7, the majority of the students rated their skill as being fair, good, or very

TABLE 4. How do you rate your research skills overall?

Ratings	Likert (N=24)	VAS (N=26)
Very Poor	0	0
Poor	0	2
Fair	8	4
Good	11	10
Very Good	4	10
Excellent	1	0

TABLE 5. How do you rate your skills in conducting library research at the graduate level?

Ratings	Likert (N=24)	VAS (N=26)
Very Poor	1	1
Poor	1	2
Fair	8	5
Good	7	6
Very Good	7	12
Excellent	0	0

TABLE 6. How do you rate your ability to judge the quality of information from print or electronic sources?

Ratings	Likert (N=24)	VAS (N=26)
Very Poor	0	0
Poor	0	0
Fair	4	0
Good	10	12
Very Good	9	12
Excellent	1	2

good. A small number of students indicated less confidence in this skill area.

There was some variation in terms of how they rated their overall skills as compared to rating the library research skills needed for graduate level work. However, many of them were confident in judging quality of information. Two of the factors that may have influenced their confidence may have been their contact with librarians or having had some form of library instruction. As noted earlier, it was found that 88%

TABLE 7. How do you rate your skills in finding high quality information on narrow topics?

Ratings	Likert (N=24)	VAS (N=26)
Very Poor	0	2
Poor	2	4
Fair	11	5
Good	5	6
Very Good	6	9
Excellent	0	0

of the students had been in contact with a librarian or had some form of bibliographic instruction within the last year. This familiarity with the library system would have likely influenced the students as they completed the survey.

Demonstrated Research Readiness

In addition to learning how the students perceived their skills, the researchers also wanted to see if the students could demonstrate research readiness. The majority of the students demonstrated competency in identifying a scholarly journal and the information required in the citation as is illustrated by the following data. First, 90% of the students correctly identified which article from a list included a thorough review of existing research on learning disabilities. Second, the majority of the students were able to identify which sources of information were *not* scholarly or academic. The challenge for them was to determine which sources *were* scholarly or academic. For example, 94% were able to identify the *Journal of Law and Economics* as being scholarly or academic, but only 46% of the students identified *Harvard Business Review* as being scholarly. Third, when asked to identify which source of information would be best to use when quoting information on impact of vehicle emissions on air quality, 84% correctly chose a peer-reviewed journal article. Students were able to demonstrate their understanding of the value of scholarly journals and the information needed to identify them.

Being able to conduct effective searches using the Internet, Online Public Access Catalogue (OPAC) and/or article index databases is a critical skill for graduate students. It was found that 94% of the students selected the correct answer to the question asking if searching for a specific keyword (e.g., provincial) in an online library catalogue is most likely to provide an overwhelmingly large list of resources on a variety of topics associated with this keyword.

One of the areas that resulted in a lower level of competency was the use of Boolean operators. The question asked students to select the statement that would retrieve the most documents in an online library catalogue using various Boolean operators. The results showed that only 52% of the students selected the correct answer.

Student responses to the questions indicated that they used both the library and the Internet for their research. From the results, Table 8 shows that 82% recognized the need to use more than Web search engines to find the information.

Savvy use of the Internet requires students to apply various techniques to locate relevant information for their research. Without this, results are often disappointing. Students were asked to determine if the quality of information found using Internet search engines is usually higher than that found in the library. The results showed that 46% of the students strongly disagreed, 26% disagreed and 18% somewhat disagreed with this statement. Therefore, 90% of the students believed that quality of information found in the library is more trustworthy.

DISCUSSION

The purpose of this study was to investigate the gap between faculty and librarians' assumptions about graduate students' prior knowledge and the graduate students' beliefs and performance. Using a slightly modified version of the Research Readiness Self-Assessment tool the study was designed to assess students' knowledge and feelings of confidence and demonstrated abilities in conducting library and Web-based research.

The researchers expected that participants would overestimate the value of the Internet as a source of academically reputable information and would have a limited understanding of the complex nature of online academic research. The opposite was found in this study. The students who decided to participate in the study exhibited a higher level of both competence and confidence than the investigators expected. The majority of participants were comfortable with technology and demonstrated through their response that they knew how to access scholarly material through the library catalogue. This has challenged to some degree the

TABLE 8. More often than not, I can find exactly what I want for my research assignments by using only Web search engines.

Ratings	Likert (N=24)	VAS (N=26)
Strongly disagree	9	20
Disagree	6	3
Somewhat disagree	2	1
Somewhat agree	7	1
Agree	0	1
Strongly agree	0	0

researchers' assumptions and own experience working with graduate students.

From reviewing the data and reflecting on the researchers' practice, three issues have emerged. First, who are the students who completed the online assessment? Are they people who are comfortable and confidant searching OPACs and who can conduct rigorous academic searches? Are graduate students who did not complete the assessment the individuals who most require assistance from their professors or librarians to learn how and where to access academic sources for their graduate work?

Second, the majority of the participants indicated that they felt competent and had confidence in their abilities to select and search academic resources. Do they have the skill set necessary to conduct rigorous and complex searches and to increase the precision of their search results? For example, can they determine what databases to search, understand the effect of using advanced search features, and challenge what they find by triangulating their search using other means? Or are the participants satisfied with what they know and can find? Is it a matter of what you don't know won't hurt you?

Third, given the baseline information gleaned from this study, do we as professors and librarians need to examine our current practices and find ways to better meet the particular research needs of graduate students? Is it possible that many incoming graduate students do have most of the skills they need to do rigorous academic library and Internet searches? As professors who expect students to conduct academic work, do we need to do more to educate students to be discerning consumers of information or have we underestimated their actual knowledge? What needs to be explained early in their programs to help them to be critical thinkers and effective in their information searches? As librarians, how do we help students to move beyond basic primary search techniques and push further into advanced searches that explore the various library resources with increased precision and results? Do we move to just-in-time training from the scheduled sessions many librarians have been offering?

IMPLICATIONS AND DIRECTIONS FOR FUTURE RESEARCH

First, consideration needs to be given to the re-design of the data collection procedures. The researchers were disappointed with the low response rate for the RRSA (19.1%). Two factors need to be examined in terms of the low response rate: what is known in the literature of responses to online surveys and the context in which surveys are administered. With surveys, Sax, Gilmartin, and Bryant (2003) claim "response rates are probably more dependent on the population sampled than on any other factor. Most studies have shown that paper-and-pencil surveys elicit a higher response rate among college students than do online surveys" (p. 411). They found that Web-only surveys without incentives had a response rate of 19.8%, which is similar to this study's response rate. In addition, they suspected the "low response rate is due in part to the length of the survey" (p. 423). Both these items may have contributed to the response rate of this study.

In terms of the context for which the assessment was administered, the ethics requirements did not allow the researchers to request that participants complete the online assessment during class time. As a result, students were to complete the RRSA at a time convenient to them. However, according to Ivanitskaya, O'Boyle, and Casey (2006), when the RRSA was administered at other institutions, usually during class time, the response rates have been as high as 77%. Based on this information, consideration needs to be given to when and where the online survey is administrated to encourage a greater response rate.

Given the research design, the researchers have considered how to strengthen the study by using a sequential mixed methods approach to gather both quantitative and qualitative data. According to Creswell (2003) this sequential procedure has the researchers seeking "to elaborate on or expand the findings of one method with another method . . . the study may begin with a quantitative method in which theories or concepts are tested, to be followed by a qualitative method involving detailed exploration with a few cases or individuals" (p. 16). In a future study, the researchers would follow up the RRSA data collection through individual or focus group interviews with participants to explore in more depth the research readiness skills of these individuals, the gaps to be addressed to enhance their skill set and what supports and resources need to be in place to foster research readiness in graduate students.

Second, based on the results of the study, the graduate students demonstrated they have a greater understanding and skill set to conduct library and online research to support their graduate work than the researchers expected. Their familiarity with the databases and search techniques may be attributed to their experience with their course work and/or with contact with librarians. However, a disconnect continues to exist between what was found in the data and what the researchers encounter in their work with graduate students. Why? There is a need to conduct further research to explore the disconnect. One recommendation is to use a multi-method research approach where the online survey would be followed up using individual and/or focus group interviews to elicit greater detail and insight of the actual research performance of graduate students.

Must librarians confront the possibility that pervasive use of the Internet and the homogenization of search software programs has given graduate students most of the experience they need to function as researchers? Perhaps they do not always operate at the highest level, but they know enough to be satisfied with what they can find. Perhaps the need for the intervention of an information literacy program has diminished considerably, leaving academic librarians to function as occasional advisers upon request. Much has been written lately about the significant changes information technology has brought to the work of academic librarians. Have librarians clung to the life jacket of information literacy as a means of justifying their positions? Joseph Janes (2004) suggests that librarians must cope with the "good enough" (p. 535) mentality that Web searching encourages.

CONCLUSION

Given the major financial investment in library infrastructure and the exponential growth of the digital library environment, how can graduate students ensure that they have the requisite research skills to be truly effective? When students enroll in a graduate program, what do they know about searching for information for their research? Based on their demonstrated knowledge, how do librarians design programs, information literacy training, and support structures to nurture the quality of research they are able to do using appropriate sources? Is there really a need for this type of support? Directions for future research are suggested.

It is apparent that much more work needs to be done either to confirm the conclusions of the current project or to confirm the less enthusiastic assumptions with which the researchers began. Evidently, online surveys may not work so other methods such as focus groups or structured interviews should be considered. If other research confirms a generally high level of research skills in graduate students, the role of reference and instruction librarians may be called into question.

REFERENCES

Bocci, J., Eastman, J.K., & Swift, C.O. (2004). Retaining the online learner: Profile of students in an online MBA program and implications for teaching them. *Journal of Education for Business,79(4)*, 245-253.

Bodi, S. (2002). How do we bridge the gap between what we teach and what they do? Some thoughts on the place of questions in the process of research. *The Journal of Academic Librarianship, 28(3)*, 109-114.

Brown, J. S. (2000). Growing up digital. *Change, 32(2)*, 10-20.

Cresswell, J. W. (2003). *Research design: Qualitative, quantitative and mixed methods approaches* (2nd ed.). Thousand Oaks, CA: Sage Publications.

Donaldson, C. A. (2004). Information literacy and the McKinsey model: The McKinsey strategic problem-solving model adapted to teach information literacy to graduate business students. [Electronic version]. *Library Philosophy and Practice, 6(2)*, 1-8.

Franklin, G., & Toifel, R. C. (1994). The effects of BI on library knowledge and skills among education students. *Research Strategies, 12(4)*, 224-235.

Gonzalez, C. (2001). Undergraduate research, graduate mentoring, and the university's mission. *Science, 293*, 1624-1626.

Ivanitskaya, L., Laus, R., & Casey, A. M. (2004). Research readiness self-assessment: Assessing students' research skills and attitudes. *The Eleventh Off-Campus Library Services Conference Proceedings*, Scottsdale AZ. 125-136.

Ivanistskaya, L., & O'Boyle, I., Casey, A. M. (2006). Health information literacy and competencies of information age students: Results from the interactive online research readiness self-assessment (RRSA). [Electronic version]. *Journal of Medical Internet Research, 8(2)*, 1-21.

Janes, J. (2004). Academic reference: Playing to our strengths. *portal: Libraries and the Academy, 4(4)*, 533-536.

Jiao, Q. G., & Onwuegbuzie, A. J. (2002). Dimensions of library anxiety and social interdependence: Implications for library service. *Library Review, 51(2)*, 71-78.

Kunkel, L. R., Weaver, S. M., & Cook, K. M. (1996). What do they know? An assessment of undergraduate library skills. *The Journal of Academic Librarianship, 22(6)*, 430-4.

Leverance, M. E. (1997). A study of nontraditional students' perceptions of their library skills. *The Reference Librarian, 58*, 143-161.

Liu, Z., & Zheng, Y. Y. (2004). Factors influencing distance-education graduate students' use of information sources: A user study. *The Journal of Academic Librarianship, 30(1)*, 24-35.

Mittemayer, D. (2005). Incoming first year undergraduate students: How information literate are they? *Education for Information, 23*, 203-232.

Neely, T. (2006). *Information literacy assessment: Standards-based tools and assignments*. Chicago, IL: American Library Association.

College students' perceptions of libraries and information resources. (2006). Retrieved December 30, 2006, from http://www.oclc.org/reports/perceptionscollege.htm.

Sax, L. J., Gilmartin, S. K., & Bryant, A. N. (2003). Assessing response rates and nonresponse bias in web and article surveys. *Research in Higher Education, 44(4)*, 409-433.

Unwin, L., Stephens, K., & Bolton, N. (1998). *The role of the library in distance learning*. East Grinstead, UK: Bowker-Saur.

Van Kampen, D. (2004). Development and validation of the multidimensional library anxiety scale. *College and Research Libraries, 65(1)*, 28-34.

Zhang, B. (1998). *Academic information-seeking behavior of graduate students in educational administration*. Unpublished PhD, University of Austin.

Associated Canadian Theological Schools: Building an Online Graduate Information Literacy Course Without a Blueprint

William Badke

In 2000, the librarian of Associated Canadian Theological Schools, a graduate seminary consortium, adapted a credit information literacy course to the online environment. With no known models to follow, the experience was one of trial and error leading to a largely successful product. The following article provides a case study of how such an on-line graduate course, with limited resources, can be mounted and maintained to the benefit of the students taking it.

LITERATURE REVIEW

Any discussion of a particular information literacy course needs to be prefaced by an understanding of theory and practice surrounding courses of its type. While there is an extensive literature on undergraduate information literacy, the literature regarding graduate students is much smaller. Fewer still are discussions of graduate information literacy credit courses. The neglect of graduate level library instruction of any kind was seen as early as 1976 when *College & Research Libraries* produced a series of studies looking at the problem in several academic library settings (Dunlap, 1976; Lipow, 1976; Michalak, 1976; Smith, 1976). Though growth of graduate information literacy instruction has been very encouraging over the past decade, the literature surrounding its theory and practice remains relatively small.

Simon (1995), in a study of 72 graduate students at Wayne State University, found that her subjects overestimated their research abilities, were unfamiliar with the library's databases, used inconsistent research strategies, did not see the need for a well-defined problem statement with a narrow focus, used inappropriate search terminology, rarely tried sophisticated searches available to them, and used very few of the wide variety of library resources at their disposal. User surveys of graduate and professional students at the University of Iowa and Australian National University have produced similar results (Washington-Hoagland & Clougherty, 2002; Perrett, 2004). While Brown (1999) in her study of graduate students at University of Oklahoma found that the subjects "exhibited a high degree of information literacy" (p. 435), the study was flawed by small sample size (N = 36) and reliance only on student self-reporting, a risky method when other studies consistently show that students over-estimate their abilities.

It is now recognized that the rise of electronic resources, both search tools and content, have made the graduate research task even more complex, thus demanding information literacy instruction of a much higher order (Jacobs, Rosenfeld, & Haber, 2003, p. 321). Barry (1997) has argued: "The increased complexity of information skills required by the electronic information world means that training can no longer be achieved as a simple one-off event" (p. 228). Yet subject faculty consistently assume that graduate students learn research skills on their own, despite the growing evidence that they often do not (Barry, 1997, p. 233; Murry, McKee, & Hammons, 1997, p. 107)

As programs have emerged to meet the needs of graduate student information literacy, they have taken several forms. Beyond the standard tutorials and seminars, some institutions have injected information literacy instruction through the curriculum (Jacobs et al., 2003; Murry et al., 1997). Other institutions have assigned librarians to graduate student supervision teams (Macauley & Addie, 1999; Robertson, 2003). Credit course offerings are a growing phenomenon (Buchanan, Luck, & Jones, 2002; Lindsay, 2004; Tobin, 2004).

Graduate students report that they prefer their information literacy instruction to be relevant to the academic work they are doing (Turnbull et al., 2003). Orr and Wallin (2001) and Drew, Abbott, and Orr (2001), show evidence that relevance-based instruction is a much more effective method than the cheaper generic models. At the graduate level, it appears that students prefer integrating their information literacy assignment work with their own projects and that they value face to face interaction with their information literacy instructors (Turnbull, Frost, & Foxlee, 2003; Washington-Hoagland & Clougherty, 2002). Thus, if an online platform is going to be used to deliver information literacy instruction, the designer of such instruction must keep these needs in mind.

Since online information literacy instruction is much more developed at the undergraduate level than the graduate, research on the undergraduate online teaching environment can be instructive for the graduate level. A universally asserted principle is that Web-based information literacy courses need to be different from their classroom counterparts and from other kinds of distance education offerings in more traditional formats. Interactivity and skill development are key. Ascough (2002) suggests that a course that is based solely on uploading information "simply will not work online. Indeed, it becomes nothing more than a print-level correspondence course, at best, an expensive one at that" (p. 18). This view is echoed by Dewald, Scholz-Crane, Booth, and Levine (2000), Dewald (1999a), Drew, Abbott, and Orr (2001), and Hricko (2001). Linn (1996) distinguishes among passive (absorption of information), active (involvement with information interactively) and autonomous learning. In the latter, the student takes responsibility for his/her own learning, using a variety of resources. Linn promotes the idea of "scaffolded knowledge integration" that sets goals, makes visible difficult ideas and practice, and promotes autonomous learning as well as critique of that learning. Turnbull, Frost, and Foxlee (2003) argue for a "constructivist" approach (active, independent learning and problem solving) rather than didactic transmission of content that supports surface, instead of deep, learning. Templeton-Kluit (2006) supports the use of Critical Load Theory, which seeks to minimize load on working memory by eliminating all information not crucial to the task at hand. Critical Load Theory aids the building of long-term memory through well-structured learning tasks.

The literature is consistent in its call to make online information literacy more than just the teaching of library skills. Tobin (2004) points out that students often view their assignments too narrowly in terms of finding sources to meet course requirements, while the goal of the instruction needs to be the creation of lifelong information skills. Dewald (1999b) states that information literacy should teach "concepts, not merely mechanics" (p. 27). Orr & Wallin (2001) argue that information literacy is "a way of thinking and reasoning about aspects of subject matter" (p. 193).

The effort required to provide online information literacy instruction is intense. Tobin (2004) is only one of many instructors who have discovered that there is an enhanced workload in creating and running online courses, as opposed to live versions. Manuel (2001) reported that the time spent in "broader support" of students was unexpected and that the expectations of students in an online environment to have 24/7 support put a strain on library services (p. 225). This writer can attest to the fact that students generally expect a response time of 24 hours or considerably less when they contact the professor regarding a problem they are experiencing.

It is also clear that not all students are suited to an online environment that requires what Linn (1996) refers to as "autonomous stance toward learning," though courses can be structured to encourage such a stance. The locus of responsibility for, and control of, success needs to move from the instructor to the student if success is to be achieved (Manuel, 2001, p. 226). Walsh (2002) lists several student issues that become barriers to learning, including time management, computer skills, and underestimation of the amount of work required to complete assignments. Lindsay (2004) argues that students who have trouble processing text-based information without the support of audio (as in the live classroom) will not do well in online learning. Taking an online course, even when student interaction and collaboration is fostered, can be a lonely prospect (Manuel, 2001, p. 222).

ASSOCIATED CANADIAN THEOLOGICAL SCHOOLS

Associated Canadian Theological Schools (ACTS) is a seminary consortium that began in 1988 and serves about 500 students. It is a graduate division of Trinity Western University, Langley, British Columbia, Canada, a private liberal arts university with a student population of 3500. ACTS provides education at masters level for pastors, counselors, missionaries and Bible translators. The educational outcomes are rigorous and demand sophisticated research papers. The literature of disciplines such as biblical studies, theology and church history are both scholarly and sophisticated.

In 1986, concerned about gaps in the research skills among students within a seminary that was to become a founding member of ACTS, I initiated, with the support of the academic dean, a one-credit course entitled Research Strategies. When ACTS was formed in 1988, the course became a required for-credit prerequisite in all programs. It continued solely as a live offering until the late 1990s when the widespread use of the World Wide Web and circumstances in the consortium made it necessary to consider a form of delivery that could be run as an option to the ongoing live course sections.

The enrollment in ACTS was growing. A number of students expressed the hope that they could take the research course before they arrived on campus for their first semester, and several programs were making use of modular courses which involved students being on campus for only a week or two at a time. Thus Research Strategies, the online course, was inaugurated, had its first student intake in the summer of 2000, and has since seen just under 400 students complete it successfully. The live course continues to be offered, though about 60% of students choose the online version.

CHALLENGES

Several issues presented challenges to this form of delivery. First, the institution had no existing online courses, no courseware platform, and few people with the expertise to create the Web presence needed. It began, in fact, with the assistance of two students who took my ideas and documentation and mounted them on a Web site that initially was password protected. This was less than ideal, because it took too long to get revisions made and because I had little control over format and layout. After a year with this arrangement I began writing the Web pages for the course myself, still without the use of professional courseware. When courseware did become available it proved to be too restrictive, and thus the course remains on the open Web, visible to all (Badke, 2006a), though students must register and complete assignments in order to receive credit.

Second, not enough of our own library databases were available remotely through the Web to make it practical to have the course be done entirely online. For the first three years, students chose one of two versions of the online course—a preferred hybrid in which reference sources and electronic databases had to be accessed within the library building (though the catalog was available via the Web) and a less preferred totally Web-based version that used reference tools and journal indexes (such as Ingenta) that were available through the Internet. Once our databases became more accessible remotely, the distinction between the two versions of the course disappeared, though students are still encouraged to use print sources or electronic versions of them for an initial assignment on using reference resources to develop a working knowledge of the topic.

Third, the medium of the World Wide Web made it imperative not simply to translate the existing live course directly into online format nor merely push content at the students. It had been the nature of the live course to seek to follow chronologically the stages of a research project, requiring numerous assignments at each point in the process. Students would generally choose a topic for which they were preparing a research article in another course, both to build relevance and to avoid a lot of duplication of effort. While much of the flavor of the live course could be reproduced online, the live discussions and particularly the live demonstrations of research question design and database searching could not be replicated. To compensate, there would need to be significant opportunity to link to teaching resources (such as animated tutorials) as well as written guidance in the use of databases. At the same time, providing a lot of flat written content electronically was not desirable, because it does not work well pedagogically in an online environment. I thus developed a separate textbook that deals with the broader knowledge base required (Badke, 2004). The course textbook offers a print-based information source that does not have to be read online and can thus avoid information overload on the screen. More recently I have added an online introductory chapter that considers the history and current state of the information process (Badke, 2006c).

Fourth, the lack of face-to-face instruction, which in the live class was accompanied by computer projection and numerous demonstrations of actual databases, made it important to provide sufficient opportunity for online students to practice their research skills. The number of topics that students needed to deal with was increased from one to two. While the total number of assignments decreased from ten in the live class to six in the online, the assignments were more comprehensive, calling for a great deal of hands-on research. Animated tutorials of significant databases were developed. Students who were near the physical campus were encouraged to drop in for personal instruction if they ran into problems. Those farther away could interact with me by phone or e-mail.

Fifth, the nature of grading needed to be revised. In spite of the fact that a very quick response time was required, the actual grading had to be at a higher level than I was accustomed to doing in the live course, where I could go over common problems with the class as a whole. Easier approaches to grading based on the use of assignments that required only multiple choice or short answer were attractive but not practical, because each student was working on his or her own topic areas. Thus I opted for the more time-consuming point- by-point analysis of each part of every assignment submitted, resulting in several hundred words of commentary every time a student's work was graded.

Sixth, there was a concern that students would need to have a forum for interaction with one another. This, however, proved not to be an issue, because students showed little interest in it. What was much more important to them was a clear pipeline to the instructor so that problems could be dealt with in a timely fashion and so they could receive both encouragement and feedback as soon as possible after they submitted work.

Seventh, there was a preference to ensure that students had actually acquired the knowledge and skills intended in the course. This could be done through evaluation of assignments, but I found it important to establish a minimal benchmark for student work. If a student did not achieve that benchmark in an assignment, the work was returned with comments, and the student would have to re-submit.

COURSE PHILOSOPHY

"Information literacy" has, in many ways, become a term with uncertain meaning despite the many definitions and standards documents that have been created. For a large proportion of information literacy librarians, instruction for credit is simply not an option and the primary activity is the one-shot generic or subject-specific teaching session, usually lasting no more than an hour.

Given that the Research Strategies course is offered for credit, it needed to involve more than library skill development or even instruction in the proper use of databases. In this regard, standards statements like that of ACRL are often interpreted only in terms of skill development when used by instructors to measure information literacy effectiveness. Credit instruction requires a larger philosophy related to the understanding of information and information systems within the context of human intellectual activity. The subject matter is information itself, and students taking a credit information course need to be able to locate their research methodology and specific skills within the context of the production, dissemination, evaluation and ethical use of information. This is a tall order in an online research course.

Throughout the course, students are evaluated, not just on their ability to use the tools of research, but on their intelligent use of the information sources available to them. This entails choosing the right tools for the task, determining the relevance and quality of the information they acquire, and being able to identify further information sources that will fill gaps in their research. Thus there is constantly a context in mind that encompasses not only their topics and research questions but the world of information within which they are working.

The course is built strongly on strategies that operate in the chronology of the research process itself. While students may not use all of the taught strategies in any one research project, the intent is to present students with an arsenal of options available to them if needed. The chronological approach enables them to comprehend the demands of research from beginning to end, rather than simply having a set of skills without a guiding structure. Such a chronology, of course, may not truly mimic the actual research process, in which the progress may be more cyclical or convoluted, but students need to begin with a process they can learn and then adapt it to their own purposes.

STRUCTURE OF THE RESEARCH STRATEGIES COURSE

The course (Badke, 2006a) is structured in six modules, each with required reading from the print textbook, a short online backgrounder that summarizes the most significant points of knowledge required, and a set of procedures to follow. The course is straightforward in its navigation, and the assignment questions are relatively self-explanatory, even for students struggling with English as a second language (though these students are encouraged to take the live course).

A look at each of the assignments will clarify the nature of the course as a whole.

Assignment #1

The focus of the first assignment is on developing a working knowledge of the two topics (most often taken from actual assignments in other courses), developing several questions related to them, choosing one preliminary research question for each topic, and developing a preliminary outline. Students are directed to consult reference sources (print or electronic versions of print still preferred over what might be found with Google) for their working knowledge, and they are asked to summarize the key features of each topic. The concept of "research question" in this course is based on the idea that a research project is a problem-solving/issue-addressing task rather than an exercise in gathering and synthesizing existing information.

The grading process involves helping students to identify good (useful) questions and distinguishing them from questions that merely seek existing information, are easily answered, or, alternatively, are beyond the reach of current evidence. Students are also asked to develop preliminary outlines, not so that they can structure their papers fully before the main research is done, but so that they can set an agenda for what they need to cover in order to answer the question. In this, the grading seeks to ensure that the outline actually matches the research question and is comprehensive enough to address its demands fully.

Assignment #2

The second assignment recognizes the value of the Internet in providing initial information and thus the initial instruction asks students to do a search engine search related to their research questions (evaluating the sites they choose for bias and reliability). At this early stage, student evaluation skill of results found is often weak. A later assignment addresses the evaluation issue more fully.

In the second part of the assignment, students complete specified types of OPAC searches related to their two research questions, using keywords and controlled vocabularies (in this case subject headings). Here my role in evaluating their assignments is crucial. Most students understand keywords reasonably well (though they use them in inconsistent ways) but few grasp the meaning and importance of controlled vocabularies. In some cases, up to one-third of these assignments have been returned for revision of the subject heading searches because the role and function of controlled vocabularies has been misunderstood. The concepts of Boolean searching and controlled vocabularies are crucial in today's technological searching environment, so the second assignment becomes a sort of bellwether for student success in the rest of the course.

Assignment #3

The third assignment introduces electronic databases and calls upon students to select appropriate indexes and terminology in order to produce lists of journal articles related to their research questions. This would seem to be a rather mechanical exercise, but students are told to use advanced features of their databases, thus demanding application of the principles of search taught through the second assignment. Students are required to "read" databases that may be unfamiliar to them in order to determine what they can do with these resources and how they should do it. Animated tutorials for the more common databases are provided so that students have at least an approximation of the demonstrations done in the live version of the course (for example, Badke, 2006b).

Assignment #4

With the growing use of open Web academic search tools, students are told to try searches related to their two research questions in Google Scholar. Hopefully this exercise will build an appreciation for the sophistication of proprietary journal databases, but it also demonstrates both the strengths and limitations of this tool for research.

The balance of the assignment calls for searches in ERIC, an often neglected resource. Students are told that, if their topics are not relevant to ERIC, they should choose topics that are so that they can get experience with this resource.

Assignment #5

The fifth assignment has always involved evaluation of resources but it has evolved over the years from analysis of a set article, to evaluation of an article chosen from a selection of three, to its current form that involves several smaller exercises. Now the first part of the assignment uses a number of "hidden Internet databases" (such as The Association of Religion Data Archives) in a discovery/evaluation exercise. The second part asks students to evaluate a number of Web sites for reliability or usefulness of information. The results of this part of the assignment have been a revelation for this author. Students, even at graduate level, are often more swayed by the graphics and perceived signs of scholarship (e.g., footnotes) than by qualifications of the author(s). For this assignment in particular, the feedback of the professor is crucial to the learning process.

Assignment #6

The final assignment consolidates each of the research topics that students have been developing through the course. While the live class, in which students have only one topic, asks for a completed research article at the end, the online environment makes completing a full article difficult. Thus, for each of the two topics, the student is asked to provide a final research question and an expanded outline with commentary related to the content of each heading, along with an extensive bibliography of the best materials gathered during the course. This assignment helps students to see how the various parts of the research process finally come together, and it provides a good means of assessing student progress.

LESSONS LEARNED

Design Is Crucial

Students taking online courses are often initially anxious about their ability (or lack of it) to understand the instructions in the course and complete the assignments to meet course requirements. Some are not sure they know how to find the course, let alone navigate through it. Through a process of trial and error the following principles were followed to enable students to assimilate the information needed and to navigate with ease around the site:

- A minimum of information is placed on the site itself and most instruction is relegated to the print textbook.
- Each assignment comes with a backgrounder that summarizes only the information most needed in order to complete the particular assignment. This includes links to other helpful Web sites and tutorials.
- The assignments themselves are stated in point form, and students are instructed to complete the assignments point by point.
- When I discovered that students were sometimes omitting portions of the fairly complex assignments, an online assignment template was created so that any gaps in their assignment completion would be noticed before submission. Developed to be copied/pasted into a word processing document, the template consists simply of the various parts of the assignment, with spaces allowed for answers.
- While not as pretty as might be hoped, all navigation bars on the course Web site have been placed at the tops of pages so that students can instantly go from one part of the course Web site to another. Here there is an advantage in using a Web site rather than courseware–navigation paths can be controlled by the professor.
- At all points, clear language is used. The principle is to present as few barriers to understanding as possible.

The Professor Is the Student's Lifeline

The online environment creates its own distance between professor and student, even if they are not separated by many miles geographically. Students must understand that they can easily approach the professor with questions and get a friendly response in a timely manner. Most interaction with students in the history of the Research Strategies course has been by e-mail, which has demanded that e-mail be monitored every day, through the day and to some degree during evenings and weekends. The "quick" nature of online instruction means that students should never have to wait for more than 24 hours for a response to a problem and that assignments should be graded within 48 hours.

This, of course, places new pressures on the online professor, but the alternative is a high drop-out rate.

Practice and Interactivity Make Perfect (or Nearly So)

Early in the development of the live class, it became clear that students appropriate good information literacy understanding and skills only by doing a lot of real research. There has to be a significant number of assignments to enable students to perfect their skills. While there are some complaints about the workload in this course (especially from those who lack initial skills and thus must work even harder), most who take it agree in the end that learning by doing is the best method to ensure success.

The online environment, in fact, is ideal for this kind of learning. The course site can be made highly interactive, fostering the "learning by doing" ethos that is foundational to information literacy instruction.

Online Does Not Have to Mean Impersonal

Despite the lack of personal interaction and disinterest in online forums, there is still a personal element in the course. Some students drop in for a visit or they telephone. Even those who communicate only through the medium of e-mail seek to personalize their interactions with me. While not easy, the avoidance of impersonality is a key element in online instruction success.

Not Everyone Should Take an Online Class

Most students who take the online research class complete it successfully. The dropout/failure rate is on the order of 5%. But there are some students who would do much better in a live class. Their characteristics are:

- A moderate to severe problem with procrastination
- Struggles with processing information when it is only in written form
- A tendency to need a lot of personal guidance at every step of the course process
- Tendencies to discouragement and loneliness
- Very limited initial research and/or computing skills

One further characteristic I have often observed personally is lack of experience with Western education models and libraries (i.e., many international students). (For research on these factors, see Lindsay (2004); Walsh (2002); Manuel, (2001, p. 222).)

Just When You Think All Is Well, You Have to Re-educate Your Administration and Faculty

The classroom information literacy course has been a required prerequisite in this institution since 1988, and the online version has been available as an alternative to the classroom version for meeting this requirement since 2000. Faculty members have expressed their appreciation for the course's results. But recently newer academic administrators and faculty have shown a lack of understanding of the nature of the course. An opportunity to present the course's main features at several faculty meetings has led to a deepened appreciation both of the course and of the qualifications required to teach it.

CONCLUSION

Final words can go to unsolicited student testimonials upon completion of their last assignment:

> "Thanks for everything. This assignment was a lot of fun, and very refreshing to put the research together in an expanded outline. Looking back to assignment #1, this journey of research modules has made good sense. I appreciate the oversight in research methodology."

> "I just want to say how much I have appreciated taking the course. I was skeptical at first, since I'm entering seminary with a theology degree, but you've 'converted' me! It was definitely a lot more work than I anticipated but it has helped me become much more effective in research. I'm sure it will pay great dividends over the length of my time at ACTS. Thank you!"

> "Thank you so much for your guidance through the semester. It was a great course."

> "I just want to express my appreciation for the course. Even though I have not met you in person, I have learned a great deal from you and your book. Thank you."

Overall, RES 500 OL (Research Strategies) continues to be a success, praised by students once they have completed it, and still respected by the rest of faculty. It would have been helpful to have been able to build upon the work of others in constructing the course, but trial and error has led to a successful result. More assessment of outcomes is needed, though the assignments themselves measure student progress quite well. We are giving some consideration to follow-up testing to determine if students are retaining their skills as anecdotal evidence shows they are, but formal plans have not yet been developed. Most students attest to the value of the course in opening their eyes to the world of information, developing research skills, learning how to use databases in sophisticated ways, and helping their progress through their programs to be less of a challenge than it might have been.

REFERENCES

Ascough, R. S. (2002). Designing for online distance education: Putting pedagogy before technology. *Teaching Theology and Religion, 5*(1), 17-29.

Badke, W. B. (2004). *Research strategies: Finding your way through the information fog* (2nd ed.). New York: iUniverse, Inc.

Badke, W. B. (2006a). *RES 500 OL–Research strategies: A one credit graduate level interactive course in information research skills.* Retrieved October 5, 2006, from http://www.acts.twu.ca/lbr/research500.htm.

Badke, W. B. (2006b). *ATLA Religion Database with ATLASerials (animated tutorial).* Retrieved October 5, 2006, from http://www.acts.twu.ca/lbr/ATLADemo.htm

Badke, W. B. (2006c). *Chapter one–Welcome to the information fog.* Retrieved October 5, 2006, from http://www.acts.twu.ca/lbr/NewIntro.htm.

Barry, C. A. (1997). Information skills for an electronic world: Training doctoral research students. *Journal of Information Science, 23*(3), 225-238.

Brown, C. M. (1999). Information literacy of physical science graduate students in the information age. *College and Research Libraries, 60*(5), 426-438.

Buchanan, L. E., Luck, D. A. L., & Jones, T. C. (2002). Integrating information literacy into the virtual university: A course model. *Library Trends, 51*(2), 144-166.

Dewald, N. H. (1999a). Web-based library instruction: What is good pedagogy? *Information Technology and Libraries, 18*(1), 26-31.

Dewald, N. H. (1999b). Transporting good library instruction practices into the Web environment: An analysis of online tutorials. *Journal of Academic Librarianship, 25*(1), 26.

Dewald, N., Scholz-Crane, A., Booth, A., & Levine, C. (2000). Information literacy at a distance: Instructional design issues. *The Journal of Academic Librarianship, 26*(1), 33-44.

Drew, H., Abbott, W., & Orr, D. What a web we weave: Evaluating the flexible delivery of information literacy education. article presented at the *Information Online 2001: Digital Dancing: New Steps, New Partners.* Sydney, Australia. Retrieved October 2, 2006, from http://conferences.alia.org.au/online2001/papers/ information. literacy.strategies.b.html.

Dunlap, C. R. (1976). Library services to the graduate community: The University of Michigan. *College and Research Libraries, 37*(3), 247-251.

Hricko, M. (2001). Developing information literacy skills at a distance: Strategies to promote information literacy in a Web-based environment. article presented at the *TCC 2001: The Internet & Learning: Six Annual Teaching in the Community Col-*

leges Online Conference, Honolulu, Hawaii. Retrieved April 20, 2006, from http://leahi.hawaii.edu/org/tcon01/papers/hricko.html.

Jacobs, S. K., Rosenfeld, P., & Haber, J. (2003). Information literacy as the foundation for evidence-based practice in graduate nursing education: A curriculum-integrated approach. *Journal of Professional Nursing, 19*(5), 320-328.

Lindsay, E. B. (2004). Distance teaching: Comparing two online information literacy courses. *Journal of Academic Librarianship, 30*(6), 482-487.

Linn, M. C. (1996). Cognition and distance learning. *Journal of the American Society for Information Science, 47*(11), 826-842.

Lipow, A. G. (1976). Library services to the graduate community: The University of California, Berkeley. *College & Research Libraries, 37*(3), 252-255.

Macauley, P., & Addie, J. (1999). Collaborating to a higher degree. article presented at the *Reference and Information Service Section Conference and Exhibition, 1999 & Beyond –Partnerships and Paradigms,* Sydney, Australia. Retrieved September 29, 2006, from http://www.csu.edu.au/special/raiss99/papers/pmacauley.html.

Manuel, K. (2001). Teaching an online information literacy course. *Reference Services Review, 29*(3), 219-228.

Michalak, T. J. (1976). Library services to the graduate community: The role of the subject specialist librarian. *College & Research Libraries, 37*(3), 257-265.

Murry, J. W.,Jr, McKee, E. C., & Hammons, J. O. (1997). Faculty and librarian collaboration: The road to information literacy for graduate students. *Journal on Excellence in College Teaching, 8*(2), 107-121.

Orr, D., & Wallin, M. (2001). Information literacy and flexible delivery: Are we meeting student needs? *Australian Academic & Research Libraries, 32*(3), 192-203.

Perrett, V. (2004). Graduate information literacy skills: The 2003 ANU skills audit. *Australian Library Journal, 53*(2), 161-172.

Robertson, S. (2003). Designing and delivering information services to postgraduate students: A case study. *New Review of Information and Library Research, 9*(1), 123-134.

Simon, C. E. (1995). *Information Retrieval Techniques: The Differences in Cognitive Strategies and Search Behaviors among Graduate Students in an Academic Library.* Unpublished doctoral dissertation, Wayne State University, Detroit, MI. (ERIC Document, ED390394). Retrieved October 10, 2006, from http://eric.ed.gov/.

Smith, E. R. (1976). Library services to the graduate community; an introduction. *College and Research Libraries, 37*(3), 246.

Tempelman-Kluit, N. (2006). Multimedia learning theories and online instruction. *College & Research Libraries, 67*(4), 364-369.

Tobin, T. J. (2004). Best practices for online information-literacy courses. *The Journal of Interactive Online Learning, 2*(4), 1-13. Retrieved October 10, 2006, from http://www.ncolr.org/jiol/issues/PDF/2.4.3.pdf.

Turnbull, D., Frost, D., & Foxlee, N. (2003). Infoseek, infoFind! Information literacy & integrated service delivery for researchers & postgraduates. article presented at *Information Online, 11th,* Sydney, Australia. Retrieved October 10, 2006 from http://eprint.uq.edu.au/archive/00000339/01/turnbull.htm.

Walsh, R. (2002). Information literacy at Ulster County Community College: Going the distance. *The Reference Librarian* (77), 89-105.

Washington-Hoagland, C., & Clougherty, L. (2002). Identifying the resource and service needs of graduate and professional students: The university of Iowa user needs of graduate professional series. *portal: Libraries & the Academy, 2*(1), 125-143.

'Library as Laboratory': Online Pathfinders and the Humanities Graduate Student

Sara Harrington

INTRODUCTION

One afternoon, when meeting with the members of the Art History Graduate Student Association, the Association's chair remarked to me, "Why don't you make a Web guide for us?" In thinking about the construction of the online Art History Subject Research Guide that I maintain, I realized that the guide does not contain any content specifically for the graduate student audience, despite the fact that the department's graduate students are active library users. As William Hemmig has noted in his discussion of an experience-centered model for pathfinders, "With the ascendancy of online pathfinders . . . there has been a tendency to lose focus on a specific type of user" (Hemmig, 2005, p. 75). Indeed, the intended audience(s) for pathfinders may be unclear, since pathfinders are sometimes created based on institutional holdings or research emphases rather than intended audience. I decided to examine the literature on pathfinders in combination with scholarship on the information-seeking habits of graduate students. At the same time, I determined to review a sampling of extant art history pathfinders or Web guides, as well as more general library guides aimed at graduate students.

This article, the result of that examination, explores how online pathfinders can best meet the information needs of graduate students and foster advanced research. The graduate student is a scholar in training. The information needs and habits of graduate students thus necessarily differ from both undergraduates and faculty members (Barrett, 2005, p. 324). While I will explore the information needs of arts and humanities graduate students in general terms, I will specifically consider online pathfinders in the discipline of art history. Art historical research presents a particular challenge because it relies equally on textual and visual information. Art history, like many research fields in the humanities, is a discipline in transition. The nascent scholar must master research practices and learn to move fluidly between the print and digital domains. This dualism presents yet another challenge for librarians in the creation of content-rich online pathfinders for the graduate student audience.

REVIEW OF THE LITERATURE ON ONLINE PATHFINDERS

I will first review the historic characteristics of pathfinders and the recommendations that have emerged for pathfinder content. Pathfinders, sometimes called subject guides, research guides, or, in the online context, webliographies or Web guides, are often considered introductory information literacy tools. Such guides generally "list resources on a particular topic, broad discipline, or for a particular course" (Courtois, Higgins, & Kapur, 2005, p. 188). Pathfinders can thus function as both a guide to the resources of a particular library and as the gateway to the wider literature of a subject field.

No library organization has established recommendations or published guidelines for the construction of online pathfinders. However, the decades-long history of the literature on pathfinders includes wide-ranging, and sometimes contradictory, recommendations for both pathfinder content and format. In his comprehensive overview of theory and practice in the creation of pathfinders, Hemmig has demonstrated the spectrum of options in the construction of online pathfinders: they can be long or short, comprehensive or pointed, and focus on print and/or electronic sources. There are manifold suggestions for what pathfinders might usefully include. Pathfinders might begin, Eloise Harbeson suggests in an early article on print pathfinders, with "a scope note or definition . . . [that] delimits the topic for the purpose of the particular pathfinder" (Harbeson, 1972, p. 112). Such a statement answers basic questions for those who use pathfinders or locate them online: who and what is this pathfinder for, and why does it exist? In an equally early entry in the pathfinder literature, Marie P. Canfield suggests that pathfinders should include:

- targeted Library of Congress Subject Headings and corresponding call number ranges
- relevant reference works, including, for example, dictionaries, encyclopedias, and bibliographies
- classic or authoritative works on a subject
- catalogs
- subject indices
- highly relevant journal or periodical titles (Canfield, 1972, p. 288)

Online pathfinders harness the multiple capabilities of the Web, which serves simultaneously, in Marylaine Block's words, as a collection of "web sites, a medium of communication, and a delivery system for proprietary information" (Block, 2001, p. 33). The World Wide Web revolutionized the pathfinder, yet it has also demonstrated the flexibility of the pathfinder, allowing a traditional research tool to have renewed relevance.

In the discipline of art history, indexing tools and bibliographic surrogates to the literature have largely been digitized, while many important research materials remain accessible only in print format. Many online pathfinders in arts and humanities disciplines thus both identify and list important print sources as well as link to electronic subject-specific indices and databases (Courtois et. al., 2005, p. 188). Pathfinders might also include concise explanations describing the construction of useful search strategies for the recommended indices and databases, which often have complicated and varied interfaces and search mechanisms. Pathfinders should also include scholarly, content-rich, freely available Web sites. Pathfinders provide the opportunity to link to important catalogued collections of grey literature that remain fully accessible only in article format as well as grey literature that has been digitized and can be accessed via search engines or databases. Marylaine Block advocates the inclusion of information on "good bulletin boards or discussion forums" in specific subject disciplines (Block, 2001, p. 33). While online pathfinders capitalize on the opportunities afforded by the electronic environment, Block and other scholars believe it useful to expressly include in pathfinders information that is *not* on the web (Block, 2001, p. 34). In short, the online pathfinder should consist of a collection of the best and most reputable scholarly sources on a particular topic or subject regardless of medium.

The formatting of pathfinders is particularly important in the online environment. Candice Dahl has offered the widest-ranging suggestions for pathfinder format. Dahl advocates a consistent scope across all of the pathfinders issued by a single library or library system. She notes firstly that all pathfinders should be easily accessible from front page of the library's Web site (Dahl, 2001, p. 227, 237). Due to recurring problems with persistence of access to Web sites Dahl states that full URL's should be given for all links (Dahl, 2001, p. 237). Although online pathfinders exist first and foremost in the electronic environment, some patrons print out pathfinders in order to consult them repeatedly over an extended period of time. Online pathfinders should be formatted so that it is easy to print out the entire pathfinder in a single step (Dahl, 2001, p. 236). Dahl's recommendations serve as a solid foundation for an initial online pathfinder format; however, some stylistic changes to format may be necessary based on specific library or departmental concerns. Lastly, pathfinders should consistently and prominently include the full contact information for the subject specialist(s) who created the guide. (This does create the issue of librarians receiving e-mail inquiries from members of the general public. The pathfinder might also include a statement about whether and according to what timeframe the librarian will respond to queries from members of the larger public.)

THE INFORMATION NEEDS OF GRADUATE STUDENTS

A concise yet significant body of research has been conducted on the specific information needs of graduate students in the humanities. In an important article on the information-seeking habits of humanities graduate students, Andy Barrett confirmed the importance of information sharing among fellow students, citation chasing, extensive browsing and exhaustive reading, and the use of primary source materials (Barrett, 2005, p. 326-330). In this way, the information-seeking habits of graduate students are patterned after more senior humanities scholars. For senior scholars, as Barrett has summarized, "Several studies and reviews of literature confirm the 'cumulative' nature of humanities scholarship, . . . the humanist's preference for monographs and original source materials, serendipitous information retrieval patterns, a reliance on personal contacts as well as private collections, and a guarded approach to information technology" (Barrett, 2005, p. 325). Eti Herman's work on the information-seeking habits of contemporary academic researchers underscores the increasing importance of inter- and multi-disciplinary scholarly materials in the humanities. Herman notes that scholars often expend a great deal of effort "in crossing over the boundaries of their core knowledge domains" (Herman, 2004, p. 38).

While most researchers develop personal strategies for handling information, such an individualized system seems to be a particular feature of humanities scholars (Herman, 2004, p. 37). Online pathfinders can function as part of a personal information management system. This is because, at their most nuanced and effectual, online pathfinders strike a balance between the communication of information and the teaching of research skills (Dahl, 2001, p. 227). In this way, online pathfinders facilitate a personal style of learning (Kapoun, 1995, p. 96), and move into the category of self-help library instruction (Laverty, 1997, p. 66).

REVIEW OF EXTANT PATHFINDERS

To expand this exploration of the information-seeking habits of graduate students, I reviewed a selection of extant pathfinders or research guides for art history that serve highly regarded art history graduate programs. I consulted these pathfinders in order to determine if art librarians have created sections of their art history pathfinders specifically for the graduate student audience (see Appendix). The selection of art history graduate programs and library online pathfinders was based primarily on the U.S. National Research Council's (NRC) 1995 rankings of art history graduate programs (Goldberger, Maher, & Ebert Flattau, 1995, pp. 478-479). I included many of the universities from the NRC rankings, and expanded my selection to include prominent public universities, as well as one university renowned for its interdisciplinary program. All of the university libraries are members of the Association of Research Libraries. I reviewed the pathfinders to determine whether or not they contained information that might be useful to graduate students, even if the information was not specifically targeted to the graduate student audience in the guide itself. Finally, I also searched the larger library Web site–rather than simply the pathfinder or guide targeted to art history–to determine if the library Web site contained a special page or section directed at graduate students.

This review indicated that the majority of art history pathfinders do not include information specifically targeted to graduate students. Yet many of these comprehensive and content-rich pathfinders do contain information that would be of interest to graduate students. Several pathfinders included information that would begin to acculturate graduate students into the culture of the discipline. For example, some pathfinders included information on how to join listservs and/or electronic discussion groups in the field of art history (Appendix, 12). Other pathfinders addressed the expectations inherent in graduate study by focusing on the rigors of upper-level coursework and the use of varying methodologies and theoretical perspectives in art historical study (Appendix, 3, 16). Others included information on specific university and departmental regulations for the preparation of theses and dissertations, as well as how to consult recently completed dissertations (Appendix, 7). In addition to general resources for dissertation writers (Appendix, 6), some sites list university libraries and centers that hold archival and primary source materials that might support original research (Appendix, 2). Finally, some pathfinders include information on local arts interest groups and activities for students who might wish to participate in the cultural life of the area (Appendix, 8, 14, 16). Such information might conceivably lead to professional opportunities.

Graduate students may already be functioning at an advanced level of information literacy. However, newly admitted graduate students may be unaware of individual university library policies and procedures.

Some libraries have a special section of the library Web site for graduate students. Library Web pages for graduate students often contain introductory and practical information, including a listing of library workshops, classes, and tours for graduate students (Appendix, 2, 9, 16). Such pages also offer assistance in contacting a subject specialist librarian (Appendix, 6, 13) as well as offers of individual consultations between subject specialist librarians and students (Appendix, 2, 4).

RECOMMENDATIONS

Based on this review of the literature and examination of extant pathfinders, I advocate a blending of traditional pathfinder content with elements that meet the advanced information needs of graduate students. Pathfinders might be expanded or revised to include content of direct interest and use to graduate students by taking into consideration characteristic graduate research patterns. Such revisions can make graduate students aware of information, and ideally, link to or access that information directly. The following elements might appear in a standalone pathfinder or in a separate section of an existing pathfinder.

Pathfinders for graduate students should begin with a cogent scope statement of the purpose and contents of the pathfinder. The full contact information for the librarian(s) responsible for pathfinder should be prominently displayed. Following this, the guide could include a summary of research support services available to graduate students from both the subject specialist librarian(s) and the library. The pathfinder might then list dissertations that have been recently completed in the related academic department, with specific instructions as to how these dissertations can be reviewed. The pathfinder might also point to the locations within the institution that hold special collections or primary source materials, especially those of direct interest to departmental concentrations and specialties.

Pathfinders for graduate students in some humanities disciplines should contain the same types of information and point to the same types of resources as more general subject-related pathfinders, including authoritative reference works, important catalogs and indices, and key journal titles. Crucially, however, these sources and other information should be geared towards advanced research efforts and departmental specialties. For example, the art history department with which I work has strong concentrations in Italian Renaissance and Baroque art and American art. An online pathfinder for this graduate student audience should focus on these concentrations. In any discussion of catalogs, I would discuss not only my university library catalog, regional library catalogs, and global catalogs such as Worldcat, but also, in order to appeal to students studying Italian Baroque and American Art respectively, the catalogs of libraries such as the Bibliotheca Hertziana (http://www.biblhertz.it/english/home/default.htm) (which contains wide holdings on Italian art) and the Archives of American Art (http://www.aaa.si.edu/search/search.cfm?q = search%20the%20catalogs) (which holds unparalleled primary source materials in American art). These links should specifically include an annotation that explains their utility and reasons for inclusion.

Keyword searching often seems to predominate in search strategies employed by students, and it might therefore be useful to include explanations of Boolean logic in order to improve the search strings created by student searchers. At the same time, it would be appropriate to introduce the concept of Library of Congress Subject Headings (LCSH), to discuss the utility of employing subject headings in search strategies, and to link to the Library of Congress Authorities page (http://authorities.loc.gov/).

Art history, like many humanities disciplines, is transitioning slowly but inexorably to the electronic environment. Humanists have traditionally expressed some reluctance to embrace emerging technologies. It is perhaps ironic, then, that younger, nascent scholars in the arts and humanities are increasingly so-called 'technology natives' who may in fact be less familiar with traditional methods of accessing information, such as article card catalogs (and issues surrounding retrospective conversion), print indices, and the location and use of archival materials found in article format only. It is clear that, for the foreseeable future, both print and digitized materials will remain important to art historical study and research. Therefore, any discussion of indices used to locate periodical information should include not only the electronic versions of indices central to the study of art history, such as RLG's *The Bibliography of the History of Art*, but also indices that serve specific subject areas within art history, such as RLG's *Index to 19th Century American Art Periodicals*, as well as interdisciplinary indices of potential utility, such as H.W. Wilson's *Humanities Full Text*. Each index listed should include a discussion of issues related to print equivalents, as well as pre-digital versions and print back files, if applicable. An annotated list of freely available, scholarly Web sites in the field should also be included in the pathfinder.

The pathfinder should conclude with an embedded link for comments, suggestions and feedback. All pathfinders should present a clean and easily readable copy when printed, and the librarian may wish to keep a limited number of print copies of the pathfinder on hand for distribution. (see Table 1).

ADDITIONAL ISSUES IN THE CREATION OF ONLINE PATHFINDERS

There are at least two additional issues to consider in the construction of online pathfinders for the humanities graduate student. The first is the increasingly interdisciplinary nature of much humanities study. The second is the need to balance the inclusion of materials held within an institution with those materials held outside of an institution. Online pathfinders present an opportunity to serve multidisciplinary scholars from other fields. This should be noted in any listing and annotation of electronic indices and databases and particularly, of image databases, as the study of visual culture is increasingly embraced by a wide variety of humanities disciplines.

The interdisciplinarity so prevalent in current humanities study at the masters and doctoral level poses both a challenge and an opportunity in the construction of online pathfinders. An online pathfinder geared toward graduate students can identify and organize the scholarly resources that constitute the intellectual core of a subject area, but in doing so, a pathfinder may have to include resources that are held outside of the parent institution. This is perhaps to be expected, for while there is an ever-expanding universe of scholarly resources, constricting collection development funds necessitates that institutions own or provide access to only a limited pool of these resources.

The transition from article to online pathfinders has radically altered their use. Yet, ironically, the Web has also rekindled some early ideas about the possibilities for pathfinders. The early literature on print pathfinders posited the possibility for the cooperative development and sharing of pathfinders across institutions, if institutional identifying information (such as local locations and call numbers) was removed. It is difficult to determine how pathfinders might best balance the inclusion of appropriate content held within an institution with relevant content held outside of an institution. I suggest as a broad guideline the inclusion of those sources that directly address departmental concentrations, and are resources without which graduate student scholarship in a particular area could not advance. It is mandatory to annotate, however, proprietary resources that have restricted access. The current academic

TABLE 1. Summary Recommendations

Elements of an Online Pathfinder for Humanities Graduate Students
- Scope statement that includes purpose and contents
- Full contact information for librarian(s)
- Summary of research support services offered
- List of recently completed departmental dissertations
- Locations of institutional special or archival collections
- Reference works
- Catalogs (and explanation of LCSH)
- Indices
  General indices in the field, indices that serve specific subject areas in the field, and interdisciplinary indices
- Key journal titles
- Freely available, scholarly websites in the field
- Explanation of Boolean logic
- Explanation of resources that serve multidisciplinary scholars
- Explanation of included resources that are not held by the parent institution
- Link for comments and suggestions

climate presents a number of challenges for librarians, including the publication explosion, reduced collection development funding, the tendency to lease access to rather than buy resources, as well as the interdisciplinary nature of many humanities disciplines. In this environment the creation of pathfinders for the graduate student audience becomes even more important.

CONCLUSION

Pathfinders represent an opportunity to reach graduate student users outside of the major areas of librarian/student contact, which include introduction or orientation sessions, bibliographic instruction sessions, and individual reference consultations (Bradigan, Kroll, & Sims, 1987, p. 335). Indeed, as Hemmig points out, pathfinders can function as a first point of contact between librarians and graduate students, and can begin to shape users' "formative experience" of the library setting (Hemmig, 2005, p. 79, 83). Chris Maiden goes further, and states that pathfinders might encourage a kind of user loyalty (Maiden, 2003, p. 34). Lest a pathfinder seem an impersonal introduction to library research, it is also possible to use pathfinders as a way to leverage a Web point of contact to a personal contact and forge an ongoing consultative relationship between the librarian and graduate students.

The construction of an online pathfinder, it should be underscored, requires a great deal of time and effort. Librarians should thus actively market newly developed or revised online pathfinders to the graduate student audience. Attempts to proactively market a new pathfinder can include a memo to graduate faculty members discussing the new resource and asking that faculty share it with graduate students (Gratch & York, 1991, p. 8). This recognizes the importance graduate students place on advice from their advisor. The librarian might compose an e-mail announcement to new and continuing graduate students describing the new pathfinder and its potential uses. It is imperative to reach out to students in the early stages of their studies, before they leave campus to pursue fellowships or offsite research (Barrett, 2005, p. 330). Using the pathfinder and describing its components in library orientation and bibliographic instruction sessions for graduate students is one way to accomplish this goal (O'Sullivan & Scott, 2000, p. 41).

Given the effort that goes into creating and maintaining online pathfinders, it makes sense, after a period of time, to monitor pathfinder use and assess pathfinder utility. It has been suggested that, "librarians . . . need to more closely monitor how often the guides are visited to insure that they are actually being used" (Grimes & Morris, 2001, p. 75). Although methods of assessment lie outside the scope of this article, the librarian may wish to go beyond the computation of hits on the Web page and solicit feedback on the online pathfinder from the graduate students with whom they work. Pathfinders are a traditional tool that can remain at the intersection of emerging trends in the online environment. Pathfinders represent an opportunity for librarians to advance disciplinary scholarly exchange, and can also serve as a form of personalized service in an electronic age.

AUTHOR NOTE

I take the title 'Library as Laboratory' phrase from Andy Barrett, who wrote, "Several studies and reviews of literature confirm . . . the significance of the library as the humanist's 'laboratory.' A. Barrett (2005), The information-seeking habits of graduate student researchers in the humanities, *The Journal of Academic Librarianship* *31*(4), 325.

BIBLIOGRAPHY

Barrett, A. (2005). The information-seeking habits of graduate student researchers in the humanities. *The Journal of Academic Librarianship, 31*(4)), 324-331. doi:10.1016/j.acalib.2005.04.005

Block, M. (2001). Teaching kids indirectly. *Library Journal: Net Connect Supplement,* *126*(11), 33-34.

Bradigan, P. S., Kroll, S. M., & Sims, S. R. (1987). Graduate student bibliographic instruction at a large university: A workshop approach. *Reference Quarterly,* *26*(3), 335-340.

Buschmann, J., & Warner, D. A. (2005). Researching and shaping information literacy initiatives in relation to the Web: Some framework problems and needs. *The Journal of Academic Librarianship, 31*(1), 12-18. doi:10.1016/j.acalib.2004.09.005.

Canfield, M. P. (1972). Library pathfinders. *Drexel Library Quarterly, 8*(3), 287-300.

Courtois, M. P., Higgins, M. E., & Kapur, A. (2005). Was this guide helpful? Users' perceptions of subject guides. *Reference Services Review, 33*(2), 188-196. doi:10.1108/00907320510597381.

Dahl, C. (2001). Electronic pathfinders in academic libraries: An analysis of their content and form. *College and Research Libraries, 62*(3), 227-237.

Goldberger, M. L., Maher, B. A., & Ebert Flattau, P. (Eds.). (1995). *Research-doctorate programs in the United States: Continuity and change.* Washington, D.C.: National Academy Press.

Gratch, B. G., & York, C. C. (1991). Personalized research consultation service for graduate students: Building a program based on research findings. *Research Strategies, 9*(1), 4-15.

Grimes, M., & Morris, S.E. (2001). A comparison of academic libraries' webliographies. *Internet Reference Services Quarterly, 5*(4), 69-77. doi:10.1300/J136v05n04_11.

Gupta, U., Salisbury, L., & Bailey, A. (1995). SuperService: Reshaping information services for graduate students. *Research Strategies, 13*(4), 209-218.

Harbeson, E. L. (1972). Teaching reference and bibliography: The pathfinder approach. *Journal of Education for Librarianship, 13*(2), 111-115.

Hemmig, W. (2005). Online pathfinders: Toward an experience-centered model. *Reference Services Review, 33*(1), 66-87. doi:10.1108/00907320510581397.

Herman, E. (2004). Research in progress: Some preliminary and key insights into the information needs of the contemporary academic researcher. Part 1. *Aslib Proceedings, 56*(1), 34-47. doi:10.1108/00012530410516859.

Kapoun, J. M. (1995). Rethinking the library pathfinder. *College and Undergraduate Libraries, 2*(1), 93-105. doi:10.1300/J106v02n01_10.

Laverty, C. Y. C. (1997). Library instruction on the Web: Inventing options and opportunities. *Internet Reference Services Quarterly, 2*(2/3), 55-66.

Maiden, C. (2003). Pathfinder enterprise portal: A study in people, power and perseverance. *Information Outlook, 7*(11), 30-32, 34, 37.

Nuttall, H. D., & McAbee, S. L. (1997). Pathfinders on-line: Adding pathfinders to a Notis on-line system. *College and Undergraduate Libraries, 4*(1), 77-101.

O'Sullivan, M. K., & Scott, T. J. (2000). Pathfinders go online. *Library Journal: Net Connect Supplement, 125*(10), 40-43.

Palmer, C. L., & Neumann, L. J. The information work of interdisciplinary humanities scholars: Exploration and translation. *Library Quarterly, 72*(1), 85-118.

APPENDIX: WEB SITES CONSULTED

Columbia University
(1) Off-Campus Resources in Art and Architecture
www.columbia.edu/cu/lweb/indiv/avery/offsite.html
[Accessed 16 August 2006, 16 March 2007.]
Focuses on electronic resources, including Internet search engines, on-line compilations on art, and searchable databases, as well as image resources, including museum Web sites and online exhibitions.

(2) Graduate Student Guide to Columbia's Libraries 2005-2006
www.columbia.edu/cu/lweb/indiv/butler/grad_student_guide.html
[Accessed 16 August 2006, 16 March 2007.]
Includes a wide-range of information on services available to the institution's graduate students, such as 'ask a librarian,' library workshops, and individual consultations. Also points to institutional special collections as well as access privileges at neighboring research institutions.

Duke University
(3) Art Research
www.lib.duke.edu/lilly/artsearch/guides/research_guides.htm
[Accessed 16 August 2006, 16 March 2007.]
Links to an extensive bibliography of 'Art Literature,' which includes reference works, catalogs, print and electronic indices, important bibliographic series, resources on the standard bibliography in the field of art history, information about specific periods in the history of art, and guides to writing.

(4) Consultations for Faculty
www.lib.duke.edu/reference/consult.htm
[Accessed 16 August 2006.]
This page is no longer available [Accessed 23 March 2007.]

Harvard University
(5) Introductory Guide to Research in History of Art and Architecture
hcl.harvard.edu/research/guides/haa
[Accessed 16 August 2006, 16 March 2007.]
Comprehensive, annotated guide to subscription-based and freely available resources including periodical literature indices, reference tools and bibliographies, and image resources. Prominently includes contact information for the subject librarian and solicits feedback and questions.

(6) Guide to Graduate Student Resources
hcl.harvard.edu/research/guides/gradresources/index.html
[Accessed 8 August 2006.]
This page was removed on 28 September 2006. The replacement page,
"Quick Start for Graduate Students," includes both general information
on library services and information on research assistance. [See hcl.har-
vard.edu/quickstart/grads.html. Accessed 16 March 2007.]

New York University
(7) Off-campus Database Access
www.nyu.edu/gsas/dept/fineart/ifa/electronic_resources/main.htm
[Accessed 17 August 2006, 20 March 2007.]
Provides instructions for off-campus access to a wide range of catalogs
and subject specific indices and image databases. Also provides information on NYU Institute of Fine Art theses and dissertations.

Northwestern University
(8) Art Collection
www.library.northwestern.edu/art/index.html
[Accessed 16 August 2006, 20 March 2007.]
In addition to information about the Art Library collection, the page includes a section on "Research in Print and Online," as well as information about art museums in the Chicago vicinity.

(9) New Student Week
www.library.northwestern.edu/nsw/graduate.html
[Accessed 17 August 2006, 20 March 2007.]
Lists introductory tours of the Northwestern University Library specifically for graduate students.

Princeton University
(10) Marquand Library of Art and Archaeology
marquand.princeton.edu/instruction.php
[Accessed 17 August 2006, 20 March 2007.]
Indicates that librarians will conduct both library orientations and
specific instruction sessions for classes and for individual students.
Includes Web pages for myriad subject-specific library sessions.
(11) Introduction to the Firestone Library Building and its Major Services

library.princeton.edu/help/instruction.php
[Accessed 17 August 2006, 20 March 2007.]
Provides information on tours of Firestone Library, and discusses specific services for faculty, teaching staff, visiting scholars, undergraduate and graduate students.

Yale University
(12) History of Art Subject Guide
www.library.yale.edu/art/history.html
[Accessed 8 August 2006, 21 March 2007.]
In addition to art museums, electronic resources, and electronic journals, this page includes information on electronic discussion groups and professional organizations relevant to the field of art history.

University of California, Berkeley
(13) Library Services for Graduate Students
www.lib.berkeley.edu/services/for_users/grad_students.html
[Accessed 8 August 2006, 21 March 2007.]
Offers and explains library support for graduate student research (including borrowing privileges and off-campus access) and for graduate student teaching (including library tours and instruction sessions).

University of Delaware
(14) Research Guides for Art History
www2.lib.udel.edu/subj/arth/resguide
[Accessed 17 August 2006, 21 March 2007.]
Includes information on researching an artist or a work of art, electronic indices for the study of art history, as well as interdisciplinary indices that usefully serve the discipline. Also includes a section on "Historic Structures in Delaware."

University of Michigan
(15) Art & Design Documents
http://www.lib.umich.edu/aael/article.php?articleID = 241
[Accessed 15 October 2006, 22 March 2007.]
Lists print and online reference tools, books, journals, indices, and Internet resources, and includes a wide-ranging list of professional and academic organizations.

University of North Carolina, Chapel Hill
(16) Basic Art History Resources

www.lib.unc.edu/art/graduate/essential_resources.html
[Accessed 17 August 2006, 22 March 2007.]
Provides information on library catalogs, online journal and book collections, museums, and electronic image collections. Also includes distinct sections on the early literature of art, recent art historiography, and on current research methodologies in the field of art history

(17) Graduate Workshop Series
www.lib.unc.edu/spotlight/gradworkshops.html
[Accessed 17 August 2006, 21 March 2007.]
Introductory page to a series of "workshops, individual consultations, services, and resources specifically designed to support UNC's graduate population."

Ice Cream Seminars for Graduate Students: Imparting Chemical Information Literacy

Jeremy R. Garritano

BACKGROUND

While college students are often assumed to have graduated with requisite information literacy skills necessary to continue their education, the sheer diversity of library experiences seen in any entering graduate student population is enough to shatter this illusion. In addition, the perceived gap between faculty expectations of graduate student library skills and their actual skills has also been recognized (Dreifuss, 1981). Though all graduates of an American Chemical Society (ACS) certified undergraduate program will have similar experiences in terms of their education in the subject of chemistry, the library instruction they receive at their respective institutions is not nearly as consistent. The Committee on Professional Training (CPT) of the ACS has published Guidelines and Evaluation Procedures for ACS certification which includes a brief section on Chemical Literature and Information Retrieval (Committee on Professional Training, 2003b). A supplement on Chemical Information Retrieval has also been published (Committee on Professional Training, 2003a). Focused on undergraduate education, this supplement outlines the chemical information topics and skills deemed important for students to learn as they become successful practicing chemists and includes a brief statement regarding the implementation of library instruction. Because these guidelines are not as descriptive or exact as some of the other CPT guidelines, there is still a concern about the levels of information literacy exhibited by incoming graduate students. To remedy this, supplemental library instruction is often necessary for graduate students if they are to effectively navigate the rest of their education and become productive chemists.

Kazlauskas (1987) has provided a careful analysis of the various methods of library instruction that can be offered to graduate students. Her report may be twenty years old, but the four methods of instruction she identified are still valid today:

1. Library instruction integrated into a credit course
2. Library instruction through workshops or seminars that meet outside credit courses
3. Specialized instruction within a particular discipline, particularly research methods courses
4. Individual library instruction, usually one-on-one meetings with a librarian (Kazlauskas, 1987)

This article will primarily focus on the second and third forms of instruction that Kazlauskas described.

The literature contains numerous examples of chemical information instruction as it pertains to undergraduates (Drum, Primack, Battiste, & Barratt, 1993; Hostettler & Wolfe, 1984; Lawal, 2001; Matthews, 1997). This literature also touches upon similar instances of all four aspects of instruction discussed by Kazlauskas. In some cases the techniques described may be transferred to the instruction of graduate students; however, there is scant literature on chemical information instruction originally designed for graduate students. Carr (1993; 2000) has analyzed the literature on teaching chemical information and in two separate studies spanning 1972-1998, has found that 56 articles have been published pertaining to educating undergraduate students versus 13 articles discussing graduate chemical information education.

The nature of chemical information itself offers further problems for graduate students. Because of the added complexity of information needs that chemical research requires, such as structure and reaction searching, advanced skills often need to be taught to graduate students (Somerville, 1990). Korolev (2001) suggests a number of ways to teach chemical information to international graduate students, including summer programs, special seminars, and mentoring. These methods can easily be expanded to all graduate students. Also, with a chemistry library housed in the same building as the chemistry department, chemistry librarians as subject specialists are in a position to provide a variety of support possibilities to graduate students (Michalak, 1976).

At Purdue University, these arguments and rationale have been used to create a graduate level instruction program. Each fall, the Chemistry Department enrolls between 50 and 60 graduate students, the Chemical Engineering Department enrolls between 20 and 30 graduate students, and graduate students are accepted in related fields such as pharmacy and food science. Because of this large number of new graduate students requiring the use of chemical information, and taking into account their varied backgrounds, additional opportunities for learning about chemical information need to be provided.

In terms of available opportunities to learn about chemical information at Purdue, there is a one credit course specifically covering the chemical literature required of all undergraduate chemistry majors earning an ACS certified degree. This course is offered through the Chemistry Department and is taught by library faculty members. There is no equivalent course for graduate students, though typically one to three graduate students enroll in the undergraduate course each year to supplement their knowledge. There is also no other course required of all chemistry graduate students that incorporates the chemical literature heavily into its coursework. Aware of this deficiency, the chemistry library staff created the Chemistry Library Ice Cream Seminars in 1998. These seminars are similar to successful workshops created by Ohio State University for arts and humanities graduate students (Bradigan, Kroll, & Sims, 1987).

The development of the seminars required five major areas of planning: establishing their purpose, finding the best format and time for presenting the seminars, choosing the seminar topics and content, marketing, and evaluation.

PURPOSE OF THE SEMINARS

Four major principles were identified to guide the purpose of the seminars. The first principle is to focus the seminars on new graduate students requiring the use of chemical information. As will be discussed in more detail in the section on marketing, this includes graduate students outside of the chemistry department. The second principle of the seminars is to make attendees aware of the libraries on campus and their various resources, with a focus on those containing chemical information. This includes lesser known or smaller databases as well as those that would be considered interdisciplinary or not traditionally associated with chemistry. The third principle of the seminars is for those who attend to gain skills necessary to choose the most appropriate resource(s) for their information needs. While only one or two resources may be discussed at a seminar, it is necessary to acknowledge the wealth of additional resources available and to put the content of each seminar into context. This may include mentioning supplemental databases for searching or referring attendees to other librarians with additional subject expertise, such as for patents or bioinformatics. The final principle is to acknowledge that at Purdue, a graduate student's greatest information need occurs as he or she prepares for the oral candidacy examination. This examination occurs during the student's fifth semester and consists of two parts: an original proposition (OP) and the student's current dissertation research summary. The OP is required to be in an area not related to their doctoral research. This process creates anxiety in many graduate students as the OP requires extensive literature searching. Besides offering the seminars as a way to connect with graduate students before they reach this point, many of the seminars are designed to make the attendees aware of how to conduct as comprehensive a search as possible. Ackerson (1996) outlines a thorough model for accomplishing this.

Next, a variety of factors were considered to identify the best format for presenting the seminars. Because the seminars were not associated with any credit course, they would have to be as informal and inviting as possible without sacrificing substance. Also, because many graduate students, particularly new graduate students, are teaching assistants in undergraduate courses, the timing of the seminars would need to avoid conflicting with many undergraduate chemistry courses. Additionally, with six other weekly divisional seminars in the chemistry department, the seminars would need to avoid these days and times as well.

To create a more informal setting, the location of the seminars is a small conference room within one of the chemistry buildings on campus. This room has a projector, which allows the person teaching the seminar to bring his/her own laptop. This is advantageous for the instructors because they can be certain that all necessary software is installed and they also have the ability to store presentations and examples of searches for easy retrieval. The room seats twenty people comfortably around a long table, with additional seating available for up to forty students and faculty total. With everyone, including the instructor, sitting at the same table, it creates a more relaxed atmosphere where everyone is able to see each other.

To make attendance as painless as possible, the seminar operates on a drop-in basis. There is no registration necessary to attend the seminars. Potential attendees are encouraged just to show up. There is also no stigma for arriving late or needing to leave a seminar early. Again, because attendance is voluntary, seminars are kept to about one hour in length. To accommodate most graduate student schedules, the seminars are also given in the early evening, which avoids most of the undergraduate courses and other chemistry department seminars. Because many graduate students cannot make a weekly commitment, the seminars are given biweekly.

The final enticement to encourage attendance is the inclusion of ice cream at the seminars. At each seminar, a cooler is brought to the conference room containing ice cream treats such as ice cream sandwiches, fudge bars, and fruit bars. This also adds to the informality of the situation as attendees will often eat their ice cream and chat before the seminar begins. This reasoning has resulted in one seminar from 5:30-6:30 pm, every other week, during the fall and spring semesters. This allows for approximately 6-7 seminars each semester.

CHOOSING TOPICS FOR THE SEMINARS

The seminars tend to fall into two categories. The first type of seminar is resource-based, focusing on one or two specific databases, Web sites, or software packages. In these seminars the background of the resource is discussed as well as a general overview of how to use and search the resource. Because the seminars are geared toward the graduate student population, advanced features and search techniques are also demonstrated. The second type of seminar is based on a particular topic or subject, such as searching for spectra or physical properties. In this case, a number of resources could be used to accommodate the information needs of the particular seminar topic. During this type of seminar the speaker details two or three main resources that would be most appropriate for the topic and then also briefly discusses other suitable resources to make the attendees aware of their existence.

The fall semester begins with a number of resource-based seminars to help acclimate the incoming graduate students to the main resources available for searching for chemical information and the chemical literature. Because SciFinder Scholar is the main entry point into the chemical literature via its ability to search Chemical Abstracts and MEDLINE, the first seminar of the fall semester is on SciFinder Scholar. This is also the most familiar database to incoming graduate students. Beginning the seminar series with SciFinder Scholar is also an attempt to make the students more comfortable with the seminar setting. The basics of SciFinder Scholar are briefly discussed, but then the bulk of the seminar is given to highlighting some of the advanced features that are often overlooked (such as the Analyze and Refine features), especially as they relate to narrowing structure and reaction search results. This seminar is also an opportunity to show off any new features that have been added into an upgrade to the software. Because of this dual nature of the seminar, it is often well attended, even by returning graduate students.

The next major set of seminars is a two-part series based on the Beilstein and Gmelin databases via the MDL Crossfire interface. Because of the complex nature of the interface and the wide variety of search functions, the seminar is divided into two parts, one based on text and property searching and another based on structure and reaction searching. The seminars are designed so that one does not need to attend both sessions to understand the basics of each type of search; however, many attendees attempt to attend both seminars.

Rounding out the initial resource-based seminars is one on SPRESI^{web}. SPRESI^{web} is a chemical structure and reaction database created by the German based company InfoChem GmbH that focuses on organic synthesis. This database has some similarities to SciFinder and Beilstein, but because many of the graduate students have never seen this database, it deserves its own seminar. During this seminar there is additional time taken to recapitulate the similarities and differences among, and the pros and cons of, searching the three major resources already covered during the semester: SciFinder Scholar, Beilstein/Gmelin, and SPRESI^{web}.

As the end of the semester nears, the Ice Cream Seminars switch to a relatively new addition to the lineup: EndNote. With the addition of a university-wide site license for EndNote, there has been a sharp increase in the number of EndNote-related questions asked of the library staff. To further promote and support this software, one whole seminar is devoted to EndNote and its interaction with the various chemistry-related databases, as well as its interaction with Microsoft Word to help manage citations in research papers.

The remaining fall and the spring seminars are subject-based and do not necessarily follow any particular order. There is a core list of subject-oriented Ice Cream Seminars that is often given with one or two rotating in or out based on student feedback and demand. The themes of the main subject oriented Ice Cream Seminars follow with brief descriptions:

- *Property searching and data manipulation–This seminar highlights how to find chemical and physical properties, focusing on electronic resources such as Knovel and the CRC Handbook of Chemistry and Physics. The various methods of manipulating data within Knovel, such as interactive graphs and tables, are also discussed.*
- *Patents and intellectual property–The concept of patents is discussed along with multiple ways to search the patent literature via SciFinder Scholar and the online databases of the United States Patent and Trademark Office and the European Patent Office. A brief introduction to patent classifications is given. Also, unique issues related to chemical patents such as how chemical structures are represented (for example, using Markush Structures and Variable Points of Attachment) are introduced. Finally, trademarks are mentioned as they relate to chemical trade names, especially pharmaceuticals.*

- *Spectra–This seminar covers the major free online databases that allow for spectra searching as well as covering the same features found in licensed databases such as Beilstein and SciFinder Scholar. Because spectral data is spread across many resources, a number of print resources are also discussed.*
- *Citation searching–In this seminar, citation searching is defined and demonstrations are given regarding the overlap and uniqueness of using SciFinder Scholar, Web of Science, and Google Scholar for citation searching. In addition, the Journal Citation Reports are also covered in this class, focusing on the concepts of impact factor and immediacy index, and how they are calculated.*
- *Current awareness services–In this seminar two types of current awareness services are discussed: those in which you create a general keyword or similar search alert in a particular database and those that are narrower or focused on just one or two specific journals, such as a table of contents alert. The pros and cons of relying on search alerts are also discussed.*
- *Non-traditional sources of information–This Ice Cream Seminar first briefly introduces attendees to such concepts as grey literature, invisible Web, open access and institutional repositories. Next, non-traditional sources of information such as dissertations, conference proceedings, technical reports, and standards are discussed as well as typical methods of searching for these categories of information.*
- *Chemistry and biology–*Covers resources related to the interface of chemistry and biology. The major literature databases related to biology are demonstrated, such as Biological Abstracts. The other portion of the seminar deals with bioinformatics and chemistry, in particular resources at the National Center for Biotechnology Information (NCBI) and European Bioinformatics Institute (EBI) Web sites. PubChem is also discussed. Only the basics can be covered in an hour for this particular topic, but it is meant more as an awareness seminar–gathering interested parties and making them aware of resources for them to explore and try out for their own research needs.

In addition, for special occasions or as a result of seminar evaluations, additional seminars are given on specific topics. Two such examples include:

- *How NOT to give a presentation–Focuses on best practices in designing a Microsoft PowerPoint presentation as well as positive public speaking habits and tips for a successful presentation.*
- *SciFinder in industry–For this seminar, our SciFinder Scholar representative came to campus to give this seminar about the version of SciFinder available in industry and how it differs, sometimes dramatically, from SciFinder Scholar. This seminar was intended to make graduate students more aware of the resources that they might find in industry after graduation.*

Additional seminars can be given if new resources are acquired or there are significant changes to an already existing resource such as new features or a new interface.

CREATING CONTENT FOR THE SEMINARS

Upon taking over the management of the Ice Cream Seminars in the fall of 2004, the author implemented some significant changes to the organization of the seminars by creating a binder system and informational cover sheets for each seminar.

At the first two or three seminars of each semester, first time attendees are given a one and a half inch three-ring binder. The binder has clear covers with a copy of the semester's seminar schedule placed in the front cover, while the spine indicates the binder contains information from the Chemistry Library Ice Cream Seminars. The handouts for all of the seminars have been hole-punched and can be stored within the same binder. It is hoped the binder serves a number of purposes: Immediately, it indicates to the attendees that the Chemistry Library is serious enough about the seminars to provide them with a binder and to go to the trouble of organizing the handouts. This catches the students' attention and many indicate their appreciation once they realize the potential for collecting as many seminar handouts as possible. The size of the binder also will mean it is less likely to be misplaced, making it easier to find when needed for consultation. Finally, for those that do attend most of the seminars, the full binder provides a mini-ready reference collection on the most frequently used resources and topics. It is suggested at the first few seminars that students place the binder in their office or research labs so that the entire research group, both new and experienced, can benefit from the enclosed documents.

The initial handout for every seminar is a cover sheet. The cover sheet is based on a similar document utilized by Purdue University's Center for Instructional Excellence for their College Teaching Workshop series. The structure of the cover sheet is the same for each seminar, so that attendees can quickly look at the cover sheet and gain the same amount of information on the seminar, regardless of the topic. The cover sheet has five sections:

- Title of Seminar along with name and contact information for seminar presenter
- Description of the seminar
- Expectations of the seminar
- Specific questions to be answered in the seminar
- Suggested readings and Web sites for additional information

In three to five sentences, the description of the seminar explains the types of resources or topic covered as well as reasons why someone might want to attend the seminar. This section is mainly used for marketing the seminar before it actually occurs, as will be discussed in the Marketing section. For example, the Description section for the initial seminar on SciFinder Scholar might state:

SciFinder Scholar is a very powerful resource, and there are many (sometimes hidden) features and pathways within the program. This seminar will provide you with some interesting and important strategies for searching SciFinder Scholar. You will see some of these approaches in action and hopefully there will be time for sharing your own tips with the rest of the group.

The next section details the expectations of the seminar. It briefly states what attendees should take away from the seminar, and gives further justification for attending the seminar. A typical Expectations section for a SciFinder Scholar seminar might read:

In this seminar you will learn some basic strategies for using SciFinder Scholar in new and powerful ways. It will also provide you with supplemental tricks to use so you can be as comprehensive in your day-to-day searches as possible. Because we only have seven simultaneous users, it is important to make the most of your time when searching SciFinder Scholar. And in industry where SciFinder is even more expensive, it pays to become a better searcher now!

The next section includes specific questions that the attendees should be able to answer after attending the seminar. This section takes the previously stated expectations and enumerates them in more detail. Typical questions from the SciFinder Scholar seminar:

- What are the various components (databases) that make up SciFinder Scholar?
- How do I access SciFinder Scholar and how does that affect my searches?
- What are some nuances in the Author and Research Topic searches I can use to maximize my results?
- How can I retrieve full-text information from multiple articles at once?
- When might I want to change the default preferences?
- How can I use the Analyze feature to show hidden trends in my results?
- What are my various options to Analyze and Refine a reaction or substance search?

The final section includes appropriate suggested readings and Web sites for the seminar. Typical items listed may be a book or article further detailing the resource or subject, URLs for support or tutorials on a particular topic, or important URLs on the Chemistry Library Web site.

The cover sheet is kept to one page and is printed on different colored article for each seminar. This way the cover sheets also act as dividers in the binder when placed with other seminar documents. Along with the cover sheet, the attendees are given any other additional handouts for the seminar upon entering the room. Almost always this includes the PowerPoint presentation that will be given, but may also include other documents as well, such as details of sample searches, a list of practice problems, or an annotated bibliography of additional resources. All documents are hole-punched for ease of storing within the binder.

MARKETING THE SEMINARS

Because the content of the seminars is focused on chemical information resources (not just chemistry resources), the seminars are marketed to the chemistry department and any other relevant departments that would have interest in the resources and topics being taught. The most heavily targeted departments outside of chemistry include chemical engineering and pharmacy, but there is also some exposure within other science and engineering disciplines such as food science, life science, and physics. While the focus of the seminars is to cater to the needs of new graduate students, the seminars are marketed to all graduate students and faculty of appropriate departments. With the acquisition of new resources or changes in interfaces or access, it is important to offer opportunities to all patrons who may have use of the particular resources discussed at the seminar. A variety of marketing methods have been implemented since the inception of the Ice Cream Seminars.

A support staff member in the chemistry library assists the chemistry librarians with designing 8 by 11 inch posters in Microsoft Publisher. For each semester, one poster is created with the full schedule and then a poster is created for each individual seminar. The posters include the title of the seminar, speaker information, and the date, time and location of the seminar. Posters are created with colorful, eye-catching graphics and text. Though poster designs vary, there is some consistency with a border around each poster indicating it is associated with the Ice Cream Seminars. Color copies of the poster are made and they are then placed in strategic areas on campus the week before each seminar. In the chemistry library the posters are placed outside the library near the entrance, near the photocopiers, at the top of each stairwell on each floor, and in similar high traffic areas. Outside the library, but still within the chemistry building, the posters are put up in a display case owned by the chemistry library, on public bulletin boards in the hallways, and near the graduate student mailboxes. Finally, the posters are also converted to PDF format, and e-mailed to the librarians of the other science and engineering libraries so they may be posted in those libraries as appropriate.

Electronic marketing offers more avenues for advertising the seminars. The aforementioned PDF files can be sent to various distribution lists, including those devoted to entire departments, or only to faculty or to graduate students. The week before the seminar, the seminar speaker directly e-mails the graduate student listservs for chemistry and chemical engineering including the Description and Questions to Be Answered for that particular seminar. The reason for including this information is to give the graduate students enough information on the topics and resources covered and the level of content (basic, intermediate, or advanced) to be able to decide if it is in their best interest to attend. In the chemistry department there is also a public calendar listed on the Web site that includes information on all departmental seminars.

The Ice Cream Seminars are included on this public calendar, which places them on the same level as the other seminars within the department. From this calendar, the department creates a "This Week in Chemistry" document of all of the events for the coming week and this PDF is e-mailed to all members of the department-faculty, staff, and graduate students. In this way, most members of the chemistry department are in some way made aware of the seminars.

For additional exposure, the Ice Cream Seminars have their own Web page linked from the Chemistry Library homepage. This page includes the full schedule for the semester and the notes and handouts for the semester's seminars within a week after they have been presented.

Finally, the seminars are mentioned wherever there is an appropriate opportunity. The seminars are advertised at orientations for new graduate students at the beginning of the fall semester and mentioned as additional learning opportunities in classes the chemistry librarians teach, whether in chemistry or other related departments. The seminars are even mentioned to visiting prospective graduate students each spring.

EVALUATION OF THE SEMINARS

In terms of attendance, the Ice Cream Seminars have been successful. Over the past two academic years, 267 people have attended 22 seminars and the average attendance per seminar has been 12 attendees, with nearly all of them graduate students. Fall semester seminars tend to have greater attendance than the spring semester. As stated previously, the fall seminars cover the larger, more well-known databases related to chemistry. The seminars in the spring are more topical and may not interest all graduate students. For example, most graduate students have some interest in more universal topics such as SciFinder Scholar and EndNote, but fewer would be interested in resources related to bioinformatics or spectra.

Because attendance is voluntary and students may attend as many or as few of the seminars as they wish, evaluation of the Ice Cream Seminars is difficult. There is little consistency in attendance between seminars, making it difficult to track any one attendee's progress, and because the seminars are not associated with any particular class, no specific outcomes on exams or final projects can be assessed. Instead, immediate feedback on the particular topic and seminar is gathered anonymously. At the beginning of each seminar, each attendee is given a short evaluation form which can be filled out at the end of the seminar.

There are four evaluative questions and two open ended questions. The first question asks the attendee "Overall I would rate this seminar as" with choices of excellent, very good, good, fair, or poor. The next three questions can be answered by the choice of: strongly agree, agree, uncertain, disagree, or strongly disagree. The three questions are:

1. I can apply information/skills learned in this seminar to my work/research
2. The format of this seminar was appropriate for the seminar purpose
3. I felt free to ask questions in the seminar

The two open ended questions are "What I liked best about this seminar was . . ." and "This seminar could be improved by . . ." The average rate of return of the evaluation over the last two academic years is 73%.

Overall, attendees are very pleased with the seminars as a whole, with the average rating of the seminars being "very good." The responses to the other three evaluative questions are skewed even higher with average ratings closer to "strongly agree." Because the evaluations have been so positive and consistent over time, more attention has been paid to the responses to the open ended questions.

While the mechanics of the seminar are rated highly, such as the informal atmosphere and the general content of each seminar, there are specific details that a number of students feel could further improve the seminars. A number of students request a hands-on setting, while others that realize this might not be a viable option ask for the next best thing–sample exercises. Therefore, for certain seminars, an extra hand-out of additional problems has been created. The attendees can then take away these exercises and attempt them on their own at a later time.

An additional question added to the evaluation form for the 2005-2006 academic year asked the attendees to indicate their faculty research advisor. Gathering this information gave some idea of how widespread attendance of the seminars was among various research groups, especially in the chemistry department. The additional hope was to see how many students were coming from departments outside the chemistry department. While not everyone indicated their research advisor, there was at least one attendee from 13 unique research groups in the chemistry department. This represents 30% of the 43 research groups currently active in the department. Unfortunately, there were no indications of research groups outside the chemistry department, indicating the need to be more proactive in marketing the seminars to other departments. This has been a perennial problem with the seminars because they take place in the same building as the chemistry department; therefore the most likely attendees are chemistry graduate students. The buildings housing departments of pharmacy and chemical engineering, while not far away, can still be seen as an "inconvenient" hike across campus to reach the chemistry building, preventing further participation from graduate students in those disciplines.

Tracking various groups represented and casual conversations with students before each seminar have also led to collaborations with particular research groups. It was found that in some research groups, a graduate student would attend the seminar and then report back to their entire research group. This could take the form of a simple write-up, making additional copies of the seminar hand-outs for the rest of the group, or the student presenting what they learned in the seminar to their research group. Some research groups have also asked for a customized seminar specific to their research group.

FUTURE DIRECTIONS

The continual problem faced each academic year for the Ice Cream Seminars is to consider what format is most appropriate. Because many students indicate they want hands-on experience, this request would require evaluating the implications of changing the current format. If the seminars were to take place solely in a computer lab, it could be difficult to finish the seminar in under an hour because extra time would need to be allocated for hands-on work and for troubleshooting individual problems during the seminar. To compensate, one would have to consider if increasing the time allotted for each seminar would impact attendance and if seminar content would have to be abridged. Another possibility would be to start a lecture in the conference room, allowing for the ice cream to be served and a brief informal conversation on the particular seminar topic. Then the group could move to a computer lab for the hands-on portion of the seminar. Again, this would require additional time to transfer between rooms, compromising the efficiency of the seminar. Another possibility would be to provide a small number of laptops to attendees to use during the seminar in the conference room. This would require additional money to purchase library laptops as well as time to maintain them (loading software, recharging batteries, etc.). At this time there are no plans to go toward a more hands-on format, though there may be some experimentation with the format as a way to solicit additional feedback.

Another issue is whether to create a registration or sign-up system for the seminars. This might increase attendance and create greater account-ability for those who indicate an interest in attending. With the current ac-ceptable levels of attendance, there is no urgent need for such a system. Part of the success of the seminars is based on their informal nature.

Continuing to target relevant departments outside of chemistry will continue to be a challenge. Actively marketing the seminars at orienta-tions and other face-to-face meetings is important for increasing atten-dance from other departments. Repeating some of the seminars in the buildings that house other departments such as chemical engineering and pharmacy has been discussed, but has not been implemented. This issue may have to be revisited.

As always, new topics and resources will be sought out as potential seminar topics. This will allow the seminars to remain innovative and attract attendees who may not have considered previous topics relevant. New topics under consideration include ones focusing on computa-tional resources like ChemDraw and E-Notebook from CambridgeSoft and seminars on interdisciplinary resources between the fields of chem-istry and physics or nanotechnology. Further collaborations with other librarians and obtaining additional guest speakers would further expand the scope of the Ice Cream Seminars. There has been success at North-western University with collaborations among subject faculty and IT staff in a similar situation (Lightman & Reingold, 2005).

Finally, developing an official credit course at the graduate level, whether required or not, could reach a greater number of graduate stu-dents in a variety of disciplines. Other institutions have successfully im-plemented such a course (Currano, 2005; O'Neill, 1993; Smith, 1993). Similarly, an achievement by Somerville and Cardinal (2003) has been to fully integrate chemical information instruction throughout the cur-riculum ranging from a general chemistry course with 400 students all the way through to advanced chemistry courses designed for up-per-class undergraduate students and graduate students.

CONCLUSION

Overall, attendees consistently rate the seminars between "very good" and "excellent" while satisfaction with knowledge gained and format of the seminars is also extremely positive. Characteristics con-tributing to this success include:

- Offering an incentive for attendance such as ice cream
- Offering seminars on a regular basis to establish a presence within the department(s)
- Adding variety by covering both specific resources and diverse topics
- Creating an informal atmosphere during each seminar
- Offering an organized handout system to place further emphasis on information taught
- Making sure attendees know ahead of time the detailed content of the seminar in order to make an informed decision on whether to attend or not
- Marketing through as many venues as practical
- Monitoring attendee satisfaction by regularly evaluating and soliciting for feedback

Attendance will still need to be encouraged, especially to departments outside chemistry. The Ice Cream Seminars were created to level the playing field for graduate students from varying backgrounds to succeed in their library research. The continual evaluation and adaptation of these seminars indicates that for a great number of graduate students, they are serving their purpose, although there is always room for improvement.

REFERENCES

Ackerson, L. G. (1996). Basing reference service on scientific communication: Toward a more effective model for science graduate students. *RQ, 36*, 248-260.

Bradigan, P. S., Kroll, S. M., & Sims, S. R. (1987). Graduate student bibliographic instruction at a large university: A workshop approach. *RQ, 26*, 335-340.

Carr, C. (1993). Teaching and using chemical information: An updated bibliography. *Journal of Chemical Education, 70*, 719-726.

Carr, C. (2000). Teaching and using chemical information: Annotated bibliography, 1993-1998. *Journal of Chemical Education, 77*, 412-422.

Committee on Professional Training. (2003a). *Chemical information retrieval.* Retrieved September 19, 2006, from http://www.chemistry.org/portal/a/c/s/1/acsdisplay. html?DOC = education\cpt\ts_cheminfo.html.

Committee on Professional Training. (2003b). *Undergraduate professional education in chemistry: Guidelines and evaluation procedures.* Washington, DC: American Chemical Society.

Currano, J. N. (2005). Learning to search in ten easy steps: A review of a chemical information course. *Journal of Chemical Education, 82*, 484-487.

Dreifuss, R. A. (1981). Library instruction and graduate students: More work for George. *RQ, 21*, 121-123.

Drum, C. A., Primack, A. L., Battiste, A., & Barratt, E. (1993). Library instruction for chemistry students: A course-integrated approach. *Science and Technology Libraries, 14*(2): 79-88.

Hostettler, J. D., & Wolfe, M. B. (1984). A brief introduction to the chemical literature with a bibliography and exercises. *Journal of Chemical Education, 61*, 622-624.

Kazlauskas, D. W. (1987). *Bibliographic instruction at the graduate level: A study of methods.* Jacksonville, FL: University of North Florida. (ERIC Document Reproduction Service No. ED 311932)

Korolev, S. (2001). Chemical information literacy: Integration of international graduate students in the research. *Science and Technology Libraries, 19*(2): 35-42.

Lawal, I. O. (2001). Integrating chemical information into the undergraduate curriculum: Information literacy and a change in pedagogy. *Science and Technology Libraries, 20*(1): 43-58.

Lightman, H., & Reingold, R. N. (2005). A collaborative model for teaching e-resources: Northwestern University's Graduate Training Day. *portal: Libraries and the Academy, 5*, 23-32.

Matthews, F. J. (1997). Chemical literature: A course composed of traditional online searching techniques. *Journal of Chemical Education, 74*, 1011-1014.

Michalak, T. J. (1976). Library services to the graduate community: The role of the subject specialist librarian. *College and Research Libraries, 37*, 257-265.

O'Neill, P. E. (1993). Instruction programs for graduate students-Two different programs. In *Abstracts of Papers, Part 1*, 206th National Meeting of the American Chemical Society, Chicago, IL., Aug 22-27, 1993 (CHED 93). American Chemical Society: Washington, DC.

Smith, A. L. (1993). A graduate course in chemical information. In *Abstracts of Papers, Part 1*, 206th National Meeting of the American Chemical Society, Chicago, IL., Aug 22-27, 1993 (CHED 74). American Chemical Society: Washington, DC.

Somerville, A. N. (1990). Computer searching of chemical databases by faculty and students at the University of Rochester. *Science and Technology Libraries, 10*(2): 67-97.

Somerville, A. N., & Cardinal, S. K. (2003). An integrated chemical information instruction program. *Journal of Chemical Education, 80*, 574-579.

Information Literacy for Advanced Users:
A German Perspective

Oliver Kohl-Frey

THE ROAD TO INFORMATION LITERACY IN GERMANY: THE BOLOGNA PROCESS AND ITS CONSEQUENCES

The discussion on information literacy in Germany during the last few years has concentrated almost exclusively on teaching undergraduates.[1] There are several reasons for this situation. First of all, information literacy is quite a new topic of discussion for German academic librarians. Although a few pioneers tried to raise the topic in the late 1990s (see Dannenberg, 2000; Hapke, 1999; Homann, 2000), the community remained reluctant.[2] Bibliographic instruction took place in a very tool-oriented way, as for example at the University of Konstanz.[3] Stand-alone sessions were offered, called "Using the local catalogue" or "Introduction to database XYZ." These sessions were not well attended. Either the students did not know of their existence, were not interested, or were not aware of having the need to learn more about useful resources. Some local innovative approaches may have taken place, but in general, the situation did not change at all. Students rarely participated and librarians were not content. This description seems to be representative for most of the German university libraries (see Lux & Suehl-Strohmenger, 2004, p. 36-38). The situation changed dramatically at the moment when the Bologna process started in the late '90s.

The Bologna Process and Its Consequences

The Bologna process seeks to harmonize the higher education systems of the participating European Union states with the vision of a European higher education system by the year 2010.[4] The former situation in the European Union was characterized by a wide variety of higher education systems in terms of structure, duration of study, and academic degree. Now the Bologna process aims to define and implement a two-level study structure similar to the one already existing in the Anglo-American world: On the undergraduate level, the bachelor's degree includes three years of studying and should qualify a student to enter a job. It could be followed by a master's degree or a doctorate. The idea of harmonizing the European system is to allow students to switch between countries and universities and to improve mobility in European higher education.[5] This integration process has not currently been completed because the reform of the higher education system is still ongoing. Universities will have changed their curricula and degrees by 2010 and some already have succeeded, while others have not yet started. It is evident that the focus was laid on the bachelor's degree at the beginning of the process because the undergraduate level was the first step toward harmonization. A bachelor's degree in the new system corresponds to 180 credits over three years, including a thesis.[6] To obtain a master's degree, another 120 credits have to be awarded over two more years.

The idea of the new bachelor's degree is to allow students to leave university after just three years with an academic degree that qualifies them for the labor market. This was not the case in the former European higher education systems. In Germany, students normally had to work five or six years for their first academic degree, a Diploma (Diplom) or Master's (Magister artium). A shorter degree course such as a bachelor's was not previously known. As a result of this idea of job orientation, many German university departments included so-called key qualification credit-bearing courses in the curricula. These courses often include information technology or language skills, research skills or soft skills, such as rhetoric or presentation. Some libraries recognized the possibility of including information literacy as a key competence in this part of the curriculum at a very early stage of the process.[7] Various examples from the University of Konstanz will show the wide range of possible solutions.

Integrating Information Literacy in the Curriculum: the Undergraduate Experience

The debate on information literacy at the University of Konstanz started in 2002, when the first bachelor's curricula were designed and some departments asked the subject librarians for teaching assistance in the field of key qualifications. A committee of subject and reference librarians started to discuss the issue. It concluded that this was to be a unique chance to develop the librarian's position towards a more research and teaching-oriented focus and to improve the library's standing in the university. Although there had been some bibliographic instruction before,[8] a new era started at this point.

During the last few years, the integration of information literacy in certain undergraduate curricula has been forced. This has led to three basic models of teaching information literacy at this level.[9]

1. Ninety-minute stand-alone sessions in subject-specific resources are still offered in most subjects, but attendance remains low.
2. Course-integrated arrangements allow subject librarians to teach 90- or even 180-minute sessions in a seminar run by the faculty.

This is the case, for example, in sports science, ancient history or political science. The subject specialist can only show some of the most important resources, so teaching remains predominantly tool-orientated.

3. A completely new approach is a subject-oriented full semester information literacy credit course that may be integrated in the curriculum. This model is already followed by five of the ten subject specialists, who cover a range of approximately twelve fields of study (see Table 1).

Most of the courses in the humanities and social sciences are offered during the first year, whereas in the sciences, the courses are scheduled in the second or even the third year because of the different ways students learn to work during their time at university. It is obvious that the content of the courses depends strongly on the subject and the specific focus of the department, but the underlying structure of the course agenda is similar in most courses and covers the whole range of information literacy, from research strategy via catalogue, database, Internet and fact retrieval to evaluation, citation, bibliographic management software and so on.[10]

Feedback from the faculty, students, and subject specialists is very positive and encouraging. The faculty appreciates the teaching support in the important field of research skills, students can improve their information literacy, and subject librarians become engaged in teaching, valuing this new challenge. Support for the subject librarians has been provided through student assistants, who take the load off them in different ways. With this step, the library management had also made clear the importance of teaching information literacy as a new task for subject librarians and for the library as a whole. Without doubt, there is a certain changeover from collection development to a more research and teaching-oriented position of the subject librarian.

This situation at the University of Konstanz cannot be generalized for the German university landscape. There is still a wide variety of approaches between universities and libraries in teaching information literacy, from stand-alone presentations to course-embedded sessions and complete credit-courses. For further information, please refer to the overviews in Krauss-Leichert (2007) and Lux and Suehl-Strohmenger (2004) and the information on the nationwide information literacy Web site.[11]

TABLE 1. Undergraduate Information Literacy Courses at the University of Konstan*

Subject	Course offered	Time per week	Credits (ECTS)
Germanic studies	Every summer semester	2 hours	3
Romanic studies	Every other winter semester	2 hours	3
Slavonic studies	Every other summer semester	2 hours	3
Linguistics	Every other winter semester	2 hours	3
Media science	Every other summer semester	2 hours	3
History**	Every semester	2 hours	3
Philosophy**	Every semester	2 hours	3
Politics and management	Every summer semester	1 hour	2
Economics	Every summer semester	2 hours	3
Biological sciences	Every summer semester	2 hours	2
Life science	Every winter semester	1 hour	1
Chemistry	Every winter semester	1 hour	1

*The different number of credits is based mainly on decisions of the respective departments. As the information literacy courses have approximately the same workload per weekly hour, the idea of measuring workload with credits is somehow contradic

** = mandatory courses

FROM UNDERGRADUATES TO GRADUATES: INFORMATION LITERACY PROJECTS AT THE UNIVERSITY OF KONSTANZ

Information Literacy for Undergraduates

At the University of Konstanz it became clear from the very beginning of the described process in 2002 that a lot of conceptual work was needed to develop a framework for consistent information literacy teaching. Given the already heavy workload of the subject specialists and reference librarians, it seemed to be necessary to obtain external funding, especially to create a temporary position to do some of this conceptual work. The library therefore applied for additional funding from the university and the Ministry of Science, Research and the Arts of the State of Baden-Wuerttemberg,[12] which was granted in early 2003 for a two-year project period. During this period, the project entitled *Informationskompetenz I,* a prototype course for teaching information literacy at the undergraduate level was developed, as well as a set of on-line tutorials using ILIAS, an open source platform. All the developed materials are freely available on the Web under Creative Commons licensing[13] and have already been reused by a number of German university libraries. For detailed descriptions of the project, please refer to Dammeier (2006) and Kohl-Frey (2005). This project focused mainly on undergraduates because at this juncture, the new bachelor's study courses were developed within the universities, and with the integration of information literacy in the new credit bearing key qualification courses, the pressure for new solutions in teaching information literacy was extremely high. Simultaneously the window of opportunity for the library was open.

But even during the planning, conceptualizing, and evaluating of the undergraduate prototype course, it became evident that there was a need to set up special graduate arrangements in order to meet their particular needs. The library therefore applied for a second project dealing especially with advanced learners.

Information Literacy for Advanced Users

This second project, called *Informationskompetenz II*, is funded by the German Research Foundation (*Deutsche Forschungsgemeinschaft, DFG*)[14] for two years and started in January 2006. From the very beginning, it was intended as a strongly cooperative project with the Library of the Chinese Academy of Sciences,[15] which already has a wealth of experience with teaching information literacy to advanced students and researchers. Besides the exchange of materials and information, two librarians from the University of Konstanz visited the Chinese partners in April 2006, and two Chinese colleagues visited Konstanz in October 2006. Further Chinese-German consultations, including mutual teaching, are scheduled for July and October 2007. Because of the strong comparative perspective, one research trip to the United States in July 2006 and a second trip to the UK in April 2007 with visits to several leading institutions[16] took place, where two librarians of the University of Konstanz collected many useful ideas for getting ahead with our own work.[17]

The overall aims of the whole project are (a) to analyze graduate information competencies,[18] (b) to reflect on their special needs in information literacy, and (c) to find appropriate ways to inform and teach them. Besides the international focus, national developments should be taken into consideration, too. For this purpose, a range of quantitative and qualitative data was collected on a national level.

First of all, a graduate information literacy survey was carried out in April and May 2006 at the University of Konstanz. This survey is one important basis for our further considerations. Some of the results are reported in the next section. Secondly, several focused interviews with German experts in the field, especially the librarians of large research institutions, were conducted.

FINDINGS OF THE GRADUATE SURVEY

Description of the Sample

The survey was conducted as an online survey and was developed mainly within the project team, which consists of three people. A pre-test with 23 graduate students was carried out during March 2006, and the suggestions of the pre-test group were investigated intensively and the survey was modified following these suggestions. An English translation of the questions is documented in the appendix. With the help of the university administration, it was possible to identify the number and e-mail addresses of all master's students, doctoral candidates, post-docs and researchers and on April 4th, a group of 867 graduate students of the university received an e-mail with the link to the survey and an invitation to participate.[19] Three weeks later, a reminder was sent out and on May 5th the survey was closed. Two hundred and eighty-five graduate students answered the questions, a response rate of nearly one third (32.9%).

Within the sample, most of the interviewees started their university career before the year 2001 (91.3%), the median being 1997. Most of them (89.4%) studied mainly in Germany, whereas only a smaller percentage studied predominantly in foreign countries. Nearly three quarters (73.3%) of the sample already had a master's degree (or an equivalent, like the former German *Diplom* or *Magister*), allowing the assumption that they are working on a doctoral thesis. A mere tenth of the sample (10.5%) had only a bachelor's degree, which is not surprising in view of the quite young Bologna reform (see Table 2).

Most of the interviewees (75.8%) were frequent library users, using the library's services at least once a week. Nearly two thirds 61.3% used the library's physical collections, electronic resources or services several times a week. More than one half of the sample were graduate students from the sciences (53.0%), while nearly one quarter were from the humanities (24.2%) or the social sciences including law (22.8%).[20] This corresponds approximately to the graduate distribution at the university as a whole.

Information Literacy Measurement: What Do They Know?

A battery of 20 items[21] was used to obtain a graduate's self-assessment of their information literacy. These 20 items were compiled mainly by the project team, with topics such as developing a search strategy, different ways of searching the resources, evaluating results, citing, and publishing. This was measured on a scale of 1 (very high competence) to 5 (very low competence).[22] We found a high variance in interpersonal as well as in inter-topical competence grading. The highest self-assessments were given in the following topics:

1. Basic search on the Internet via search engines ($\bar{\chi}$ = 1.50)
2. Basic search in the local OPAC ($\bar{\chi}$ = 1.75)
3. Citing correctly ($\bar{\chi}$ = 1.82)

The grading of the first item is not astonishing. Everyone knows: It is so easy to write your keywords into the Google search field and

TABLE 2. Highest Academic Degree

Academic degree	n	%
Bachelor's	30	10.5
Master's, Magister, Diplom etc.	209	73.3
Dr., PhD, *Habilitation*	34	11.9
Other (e.g. Swiss *Lizenziat*)	12	4.2
Total	**285**	**100**

click on "I'm feeling lucky." In conjunction with another result of the survey, the picture becomes even more interesting. When we asked which sources the interviewees usually used for the investigation of specific research results (see Figure 1), the overwhelming answer was search engines, and most likely that means Google. That means that most of the graduate students search for current research results with the tool they think they can handle best: Google. These facts lead to the already ongoing discussion that libraries and database providers should make more effort to make their search interfaces even more frugal and to integrate more bibliographic data into the search engines.

The average personal information literacy assessment, calculated as an index for each graduate student, including the 20 items, is $\bar{\chi}$ =2.62. The variance of this self-assessment as a whole, graded between "high" and "neutral," is extremely high (see Figure 2). Further conclusions are discussed in the next section.

Information Literacy Ignorance: What to Teach Them?

One obvious starting point for the needs of the graduate students is their self-assessment. The six lowest rated items according to this are:

15. Use of bibliographic management software ($\bar{\chi}$ = 2.80)
16. Usage of optional search parameters ($\bar{\chi}$ = 2.84)

FIGURE 1. Which sources do you use for the investigation of specific research results?

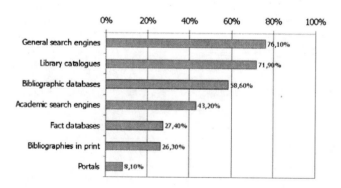

FIGURE 2: Self-Assessment of Information Literacy

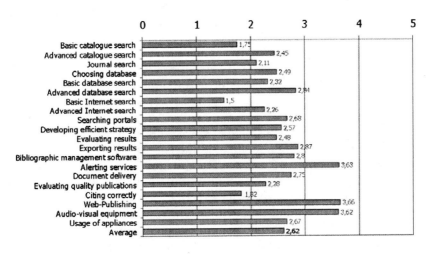

17. Exporting of search results ($\overline{\chi}$ = 2.87)
18. Audio-visual equipment ($\overline{\chi}$ = 3.62)
19. Alerting services ($\overline{\chi}$ = 3.63)
20. Web publishing, e.g., institutional repository *($\overline{\chi}$ = 3.66)*

So it is particularly the more sophisticated functions of search instruments (optional search parameters like truncation, index search, etc., the export of data and the initializing of alerting services) that are named as necessary competence extensions. The use of bibliographic management software seems to fit very properly into this whole field of advanced searching, exporting and managing references, and staying up to date, which could be the focus of a workshop, a series of workshops or an important part of a semester-long course in information literacy for advanced users.

The use of audio-visual equipment (video digitalization, film cutting, preparation of audio-visual teaching material, etc.), however, is expected to be the need of a very specific target group, such as media scientists or historians, working with that sort of material. For them, custom-made solutions could be provided.

The self-publishing of research papers, especially on an institutional repository (like *KOPS*, the Konstanz Online Publication System), is a requirement, too. At the moment, the library is particularly active in promoting this form of academic publishing as the "green way" of the Open Access movement. One-on-one support is already provided, but with the results of the self-assessment, workshops should also be considered. Besides the information literacy self-assessment, the survey points to at least one more lack of competence: the above-mentioned result that most of the interviewees use general search engines for the search of current research results (see Figure 1).

One can draw the conclusion that the adequacy of using general and academic search engines should be at the core of information literacy instruction for graduate students. There is no doubt that Google and Google Scholar, in particular, are becoming more and more attractive for the academic community as they include more and more content in their engines, despite all the disadvantages they imply (for an overview see Miller & Pellen, 2005). It may be that the librarians' mission is to show how they are best used and to show the alternatives to the patrons as well.

Another interesting question in this context was which services the graduate students would like to use in the future. Most of them answered that they would favor consulting in specific areas. These results basically confirm the observations described above:

1. Consulting in the use of specific databases (46.3%)
2. Introduction to bibliographic management software (45.6%)
3. Consulting in searching for academic literature (41.4%)
4. Information about electronic publishing (38.9%)

Offering Information Literacy: How to Reach Them?

If a library seeks to reach a certain target group, that means two things. First of all a simple channel of information is needed, along which the library is able to convey purposeful information to the user. Secondly, to go one step further, the library needs ways of imparting knowledge (e.g., about topics in information literacy) to the user. Both topics were addressed in the graduate survey at the University of Konstanz.

The first question, concerning the channel of information, asked how the users want to be informed about library news. The results are not surprising, with an electronic newsletter being the most requested method of information (see Figure 3).

FIGURE 3. How do you want to be informed about library news?

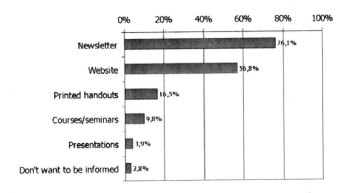

FIGURE 4. How do you wish to be advised by the library in the future?

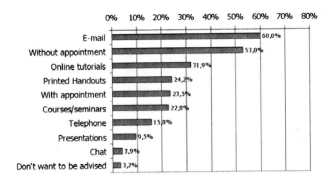

During the last years, particular subject oriented mailing lists have already existed at the library at the University of Konstanz with sporadic mailings to several interested users. One consequence of the survey result will be the creation of a more institutionalized library-wide newsletter, which will be sent biweekly from the summer semester 2007 with a broader range of content.

In addition to the simple dissemination of information, the second question asked how the graduate students want to be advised by the library (see Figure 4). The purpose of this question was to gather more information about the ways advanced users could be instructed in the different fields of information literacy. We presumed that the graduate students could not be reached as easily as the undergraduates in workshops or courses, a fact which was basically validated by the survey's results: Most of the graduate students prefer to receive advice in an e-mail (60.0%), in personal talks with the librarians at the reference desk without appointment (53.0%), and with the help of online-tutorials (31.9%) or printed brochures (24.2%). Fewer of them called for one-on-one appointments with an individually fixed date (23.5%) or expressed their willingness to participate in courses or workshops (22.8%).

On the one hand, these findings seem to be a contrast to the statements of the experts we had already interviewed in Germany, China, the UK and the US, where we learned a lot about the importance of one-on-one consultations. On the other hand, one can argue that nevertheless, nearly one quarter are interested in such a formal consultation with a temporal arrangement. At the University of Konstanz, we will debate the possibilities of extending our service in this area, at least for a small target group. Older scholars with a higher degree are more interested in one-on-one consultations, while master's students and doctoral candidates are more interested in courses and workshops, and both facts will be taken into account in our future plans.

The fact that one quarter are interested in participating in courses or workshops seems not very much at first glance. But it is still one quarter that could be reached in this way. So the impression that graduate students are not willing to take part in a workshop or session is not completely validated with these results. Again, the approach will probably have to be changed, from tool-oriented sessions ("Introduction to the database XYZ") to problem-oriented workshops ("Manage your references," "Staying alert!" etc.).

PERSPECTIVES

During the remaining project period of *Informationskompetenz II*, additional tasks will be completed. More interviews with German and international experts in the field will be conducted. Together with different German information literacy initiatives, data will be collected concerning the graduate information literacy engagement of the large university libraries. Various ways of teaching information literacy to the target group will be tested and evaluated to come to a sustainable and successful set of methods for teaching graduate information literacy in the German university system. Some examples of plans for concrete measures follow.

Teaching Master Students in a Credit Bearing Course

From the winter semester 2006, a semester-long credit-bearing course in politics and management is the first credit course for the master's level at the University of Konstanz. It is included in the study regulations, is mandatory for all master's students (approximately 40 per year) and awarded with four credits. It is situated in the methods module, which consists of two lectures in research design (seven credits each) and the information literacy course. The content of the course, which is taught by the subject specialist for political science, includes the full range of basic information literacy (research strategy, knowledge of and searching in the relevant resources, evaluation, citation, bibliographic management software etc.) as it is imparted in bachelor's courses. During the first course it became evident that information literacy basics have to be repeated once again because transfer is not always achieved, even if the students already took part in an undergraduate information literacy course. Obviously the level of the master course has to be higher, e.g., in terms of the resources presented, but repetition still seems to be necessary. In addition, the focus will shift to some new topics, e.g., academic writing or ethical questions (such as plagiarism) or will be more intensive in some more common fields, e.g., the most relevant resources from adjacent subjects (such as law) or the use of bibliographic management software (which is more necessary for graduate students). To meet the needs of students, the course looked at their fields of interest and the content depended strongly on their previous knowledge. During the course, the information literacy of the 32 participants increased by 8%, measured with a simple test before and after the term. The self-assessment of the students even increased by 12.5%.[23]

Since the development of the master's curricula at the German universities is still "work in progress," with the first degree courses just now starting, this master's course was equally "work in progress." Further courses on the graduate level at the University of Konstanz, e.g., in sports sciences from the winter semester 2007, will highly profit from these experiences.

Collaborating with Doctoral Research Training Groups

The University of Konstanz has a strong tradition of supporting and promoting young scholars. At the University of Konstanz, several research training groups for doctoral students (*Graduiertenkollegs*) are working with postgraduates on campus. In addition to the existing four groups from the sciences, social sciences and humanities, a fifth group was established in spring 2006 in cooperation with the University of Zurich, the Swiss Federal Institute of Technology (ETH Zurich) and two pharmaceutical companies, doing research in the sciences. Close collaboration with the instruction librarian for the sciences was arranged to offer information literacy workshops for the doctoral candidates. Workshops on research strategy, relevant resources, or bibliographic management software will be provided by the library from 2007 onwards.

New Services for a Certain Target Group

Some years ago, the University of Konstanz founded a Centre for Junior Research Fellows (*Zentrum für den Wissenschaftlichen Nachwuchs*) to attract excellent young scholars to the university. The university intends to strengthen and broaden the importance of the junior scholars within the current German excellence initiative of the German Research Foundation (*Exzellenzinitiative* of the *DFG*). The aim of the initiative is to promote top-level research and to improve the quality of German universities. Therefore 1.9 billion will be spent (2006-2011) in three lines of funding, and the DFG will come to a final decision in October 2007. The University of Konstanz has applied for funding in this initiative with a focus on junior scholars to enlarge the Centre for Junior Research fellows. Hence the library is debating tailor-made support for young scholars, and the members of the Centre have been selected as a first group to profit from these services. After an initial discussion with the members of the Centre a first concept has been developed to support these researchers: Several information literacy workshops, dealing with bibliographic management software or open access publishing, will be realized from the summer term 2007. In addition, the role of the subject librarian as a personal librarian for this target group is emphasized more: From the beginning of 2007 a welcoming one-on-one consultation is offered to every new member of the Centre.

Training the Faculty as Multipliers

A completely different approach is to train the faculty so that they are able to teach students in information literacy in their courses. This concept of bringing the faculty on board is not a new one in the information literacy debate, but we are trying to walk a new road: In the state of Baden-Wuerttemberg with its nine universities, a Centre for Higher Education Didactics (*Hochschuldidaktikzentrum, HDZ*) was founded a few years ago to support young scholars in particular in improving their university teaching by means of special workshops in teaching methods, course planning, assignments and so on. In 2007, two new one-day workshops are offered within this Centre. One course on information literacy and e-learning has already taken place in January. Afterwards several participants have uttered their intention to integrate e-learning in their own teaching. Another course on ethics and plagiarism will be provided by librarians of the University of Konstanz for all interested faculty members in Baden-Wuerttemberg in July. Our aim is to impart basic knowledge in information literacy and customized methods for integrating information literacy into the curriculum of the faculty's courses.

International Symposium on Graduate Information Literacy

As the final stage of the *Informationskompetenz II* project, an international symposium on graduate information literacy is planned to be held at the University of Konstanz, probably in winter 2007/08. We intend to invite international experts in the field to give a state-of-the-art report and to initiate a constructive debate in this important area of librarianship.

CONCLUSION

The Konstanz graduate survey provides useful results for the further development of information literacy services for graduate students. The most important findings are that the graduate's information literacy competencies could be improved in certain fields using different ways and methods of information and advice. The University of Konstanz library has already developed and implemented varying models of information literacy instruction and consulting for graduate students and will extend these services in the future. The library took the opportunities that arose out of the Bologna process, especially with the formal integration of information literacy courses in Bachelor's and Master's curricula. In contrast, not only the needs of doctoral students and post-docs are different, but also their institutional integration is less formalized. That led to a different library strategy with customized services and close relationships with doctoral research training groups or the Centre for Junior Research Fellows. The cooperation with such institutions seems to facilitate the achievement of our goal to improve the library's information literacy services and the graduate students' information literacy competencies.

NOTES

1. As a German term for information literacy, Informationsliteralitaet is not used, because the word Literalitaet is not widely used in the German language. Instead, the German discussion uses the term Informationskompetenz (information competence). For an overview see Krauss-Leichert (2007) and Lux & Sühl-Strohmenger (2004).

2. Hence, there have been no national information literacy standards as exist in the Anglo-American world up to now. There have, however, been some regional campaigns, often based on ACRL standards, to develop regional standards. There will probably be integration in a national standard, but this is an open-ended process. The discussion is still continuing. For the region of Baden-Wuerttemberg, see: www.informationskompetenz.de/fileadmin/DAM/documents/Standards%20der%20Inform_88.pdf (April 13, 2007).

3. The University of Konstanz is one of the smaller universities in the south-western German state of Baden-Wuerttemberg. The young university was founded in 1966 and has approximately 10,400 students and 1,140 staff in total, whereof 174 are full-time professors. The library has an open stack collection of 2 million volumes and is open nearly 24/7 (141 hours per week). A staff of 95 works for the library, including ten subject specialists. They have tenure positions, but are not faculty members.

4. It is named after the Northern Italian city of Bologna, where the treaty was signed in 1999 by the responsible ministers of education from 29 European states. For further information, see Reinalda and Kulesza (2005).

5. For further information, please visit the Web site of the current Bologna Secretariat: www.dfes.gov.uk/bologna/ (April 13, 2007).

6. The European Credit Transfer System (ECTS) sets an average workload of 30 hours for one credit, which means a workload of 180 * 30 hours (= 5,400 hours). Therefore not every course or lecture is valued with the same number of credits per hour of teaching, since it also depends on the time for preparation and post processing of the course or lecture. Hence this varies widely from one to approximately eight or even more credits.

7. A second very important reason for the rise of the information literacy debate was the publication of the so-called SteFi-Studie in the year 2001 (Klatt, Gavriilidis, Kleinsimlinghaus, & Feldmann, 2001). This study analyzed the information competencies of students and faculty members in a nation-wide survey. The findings were dramatic.

8. Besides the above-mentioned stand-alone sessions, there had already been a full semester research skills course in philosophy and various lectures, mainly for Germanic studies.

9. Again, besides the non subject specific one hour workshops, such as an introduction to the catalogue, to Internet searching or bibliographic management software.

10. For the detailed content of the courses see Dammeier (2006).

11. www.informationskompetenz.de.

12. www.mwk-bw.de.

13. See: http://www.ub.uni-konstanz.de/bibliothek/projekte/informationskompetenz.html.

14. www.dfg.de.

15. www.las.ac.cn/en.

16. We are very grateful to Columbia, NYU, MIT, Yale, Stanford, UC Berkeley, UCLA, University of Sheffield, Manchester Metropolitan University, Imperial Col-

lege London and London Metropolitan University for their hospitality and openness. A report including the findings is in preparation.

17. More information can be found on the Web: http://www.ub.uni-konstanz. de/bibliothek/projekte/informationskompetenz.html.

18. A comprehensive literature review regarding graduate student's information literacy is in preparation and will be published later this year.

19. This has led to two biases: The first bias is that only graduate students with a registered e-mail account had the chance to participate in the survey. The second bias is that only master and doctoral students and post-docs had the chance to participate, but not the 4th and 5th year students of the former Diplom studies. The reason is that it would have been very complicated to look them up in the university administration's database, so they were excluded from the target group, as well as the people without a registered e-mail account.

20. There is no medical or engineering department at the University of Konstanz.

21. Following the existing standards of information literacy.

22. The methodological problems of a subjective self-assessment in this way are known as social desirability effects (see Diekmann, 1995, p.382-385). But given these problems, it is an adequate measurement of self-assessment, which was used in much larger relevant surveys, e.g., Klatt, Gavriilidis, Kleinsimlinghaus, & Feldmann (2001). A more objective measurement of the information literacy of a certain group could be done with questions as were developed by the SAILS project, for example, (www. projectsails.org). A step in this direction was made during the graduate course in political science, see the chapter "Perspectives."

23. Source: Own data and calculations.

BIBLIOGRAPHY

Dammeier, J. (2006). Informationskompetenz mit Blended Learning: Ergebnisse des Projekts Informationskompetenz I der Bibliothek der Universität Konstanz. *Bibliotheksdienst, 40* (3), 314-330.

Dannenberg, D. (2000). Wann fangen Sie an? Das Lernsystem Informationskompetenz (LIK) als praktisches Beispiel einer Teaching Library. *Bibliotheksdienst, 34* (7/8), 1245-59.

Diekmann, A. (1995): *Empirische Sozialforschung: Grundlagen, Methoden, Anwendungen.* Reinbek: Rowohlt.

Hapke, T. (1999). Recherchestrategien in elektronischen Datenbanken: Inhaltliche Elemente der Schulung von Informationskompetenz (nicht nur) an Universitätsbibliotheken. *Bibliotheksdienst, 33* (7), 1113-1129.

Homann, B. (2000). Informationskompetenz als Grundlage für bibliothekarische Schulungskonzepte. *Bibliotheksdienst, 34* (6), 968-997.

Klatt, R., Gavriilidis, K., Kleinsimlinghaus, K., & Feldmann, M. et al. (2001). *Nutzung elektronischer wissenschaftlicher Information in der Hochschulausbildung: Barrieren und Potenziale der innovativen Mediennutzung im Lernalltag der Hochschulen (Endbericht).* Dortmund.

Kohl-Frey, O. (2005). *Modularisierung,* E-Learning und die Einbindung in Studienpläne: Zur Vermittlung von Informationskompetenz an der Universität Konstanz. *Bibliothek, 29* (1), 42-48.

Krauss-Leichert, U. (Ed.) (2007). *Teaching Library: eine Kernaufgabe für Bibliotheken.* Frankfurt: Lang.
Lux, C., & Suehl-Strohmenger, W. (2004). *Teaching Library in Deutschland.* Wiesbaden: Dinges und Frick.
Miller, W., & Pellen, R. M. (Eds.) (2005). *Libraries and Google.* Binghamton, NY: Haworth Information Press.
Reinalda, B., & Kulesza, E. (2005). *The Bologna process: harmonizing Europe's higher education.* Opladen: Budrich.

APPENDIX. Translation of the graduate survey at the University of Konstanz (During translation, some questions were slightly changed to avoid some typical German expressions which are not necessary in this context.)

1. In which year did you start your first course of studies at a university?
2. Where have you attended university for most of the time?
   • Germany
   • United Kingdom or Ireland
   • Middle, Western or Southern Europe
   • Northern Europe
   • Eastern Europe
   • USA, Canada, Australia or New Zealand
   • Middle or South America
   • Africa
   • Asia
3. Which is the highest academic grade you have obtained?
   • B.A., BSc, etc.
   • M.A., Magister, Diplom, etc.
   • Dr., PhD
   • Habilitation
   • Professor
   • None
   • Other
4. In which function do you mainly use the Library of the University of Konstanz ?
   • Student
   • Employee (non researcher w/o tenure)
   • Employee (researcher w/o tenure)
   • Scholarship holder, member of a graduate school, etc.

- External user
- Visiting lecturer
- Other

5. How often do you use the services of the library (e.g., lending, catalogue search and using databases, document delivery)?
- Several times a week
- About once a week
- Several times a month
- About once a month
- Fewer
- Never

6. To which department do you attribute yourself?
- Mathematics and Statistics
- Informatics und Information Sciences
- Physics
- Chemistry
- Biology
- Psychology
- Philosophy
- History
- Sociology, Sports, Pedagogies
- Literature, Art and Media Sciences
- Linguistics
- Law
- Economics
- Politics and Administrative Sciences
- University Administration and Services
- None

7. How do you inform yourself about new developments in your profession or field of research? (Five answers at most)
- Journals (print)
- Journals (electronic)
- Bibliographic databases
- Internet portals
- Automatic alerts
- Online contents, current contents
- Exchange with colleagues
- Newsletter, Weblogs, mailing lists
- Assignment of research service providers (with costs)
- Publisher programs
- Publications of professional associations
- Other

8. Which sources do you use for the investigation of specific research results?
- General search engines (Google, Yahoo, etc.)
- Academic search engines (Google Scholar, Scirus, etc.)
- Library catalogues
- Bibliographic databases (Scopus, MLA, Pubmed, etc.)
- Fact databases
- Bibliographies in print
- Portals (Elektra, Vascoda, etc.)
- Other

9. How do you obtain full texts, which you need for your academic work?
- Printed stock of the library (Journals, books, etc.)
- Electronic texts (E-Journals, full-text servers)
- Free publications from the Internet
- Document delivery
- Swapping texts with colleagues (PDF, reprints, preprints, etc.)
- The student assistants, secretaries care for this
- Other

10. Self-assessment of my skills and knowledge (1 = very high, 5 = very low)
- Basic search in local OPAC
- Advanced search in local OPAC
- Search for journals in local OPAC
- Choosing the right database
- Basic search in chosen database
- Usage of optional search parameters (truncation, indexes, thesaurus, etc.)
- Basic search in the Internet via search engines (google, etc.)
- Advanced search via search engines
- Search in portal-sites
- Developing an efficient strategy for enquiries
- Evaluation of results; broadening or narrowing of enquiry parameters
- Exporting results from catalogues and databases
- Electronic bibliography software (Endnote, BibTex, Bibliographix, etc.)
- Alerting services of databases, publishers, etc.
- Document delivery (print, electronic)
- Evaluation of the quality of publications
- Citing correctly

- Web-publishing (publishing on the Internet, institutional repository, etc.)
- Audio-visual equipment (video, cutting, preparation of teaching-material)
- Usage of appliances (video-beamer, vcr, reader-printer, microfilm-reader, etc.)

11. How did you acquire these skills?
- Learning by doing, trial and error
- Autodidactic with teaching material (e.g., online tutorials, books)
- With the help of colleagues and friends
- Direct support of library employees
- Courses of the library
- Courses of your department
- Courses outside the university (schools, community colleges)
- Courses at the Hochschuldidaktikzentrum
- Other

12. How useful has this method been for you? (1 = very useful, 5 = not useful)
- Learning by doing, trial and error
- Autodidactic with teaching material (e.g., online tutorials, books)
- With the help of colleagues and friends
- Direct support of library employees
- Courses of the library
- Courses of your department
- Courses outside the university (schools, community colleges)
- Courses at the Hochschuldidaktikzentrum
- Other

13. Finally we would like to know what your experiences have been with the library.
- Which of these library services would you like to use in the future?
- Help with enquiries for academic literature.
- Help with the use of certain databases.
- Help with the use of fact databases (protein databases, statistics, etc.
- Introduction in the use of bibliographic management software
- Information on electronic publishing (e.g., institutional repository)
- Legal help (copyright for authors)
- Extension of the e-learning platform (online tutorials)
- Help on the problem of plagiarism in student papers
- Research assignments by the library

- None
- Other

14. How do you want to be informed about library news?
- Printed handouts
- On the Web site of the library
- Electronic newsletter
- Presentation
- Courses
- I don't want to be informed
- Other

15. How do you wish to be advised by the library in the future?
- One on one appointments
- Help by the employees of the help desk (without appointment)
- Printed handouts
- Online tutorials and e-learning
- Phone
- Chat
- E-mail
- Presentation
- Courses
- I don't want to be advised.
- Other

16. How content are you with the library all things considered? (1 = very content, 5 = not content)

InfoIQ: Targeting Information and Technology Lifelong Needs

Jason L. Frand
Eloisa Gomez Borah
Aura Lippincott

Instruction for information literacy skills has to take a long view. This is crucial for these skills to be instilled in a students' repertoire of tools they would use naturally. When librarians teach information literacy skills to students, the outcomes they expect need to extend beyond those of the current class assignment. The best designed instruction assures that the skills taught are useful in other course work and beyond. This article describes a plan for information literacy instruction to graduate students that evolved at the UCLA Anderson School of Management. The plan emphasizes the need for instruction that develops student competencies with an eye toward the long view–a lifetime of learning.

GRADUATE STUDENTS ARE DIFFERENT

Many information literacy programs for graduate students are fashioned closely to those of their undergraduate counterparts with a focus on the basics of searching online resources. However, graduate students, unlike undergraduates, are more receptive to a longer view for information literacy skills. Their projects and research usually extend over a longer period of time and their field of concentration is likely to have recurring processes involving information needs. Their theses, thesis-equivalent projects, internships or dissertations are likely to employ many repetitive processes commonplace in their disciplines.

Business school students tend to see themselves as "born to run things" with their decisions leading to actions impacting others. Additionally, business school students are early adopters of technology and thus fore-runners of future trends. At the UCLA Anderson School of Management, our graduate students see themselves as business people coming back to school rather than as students who will someday be going into business. Our student clients are full-time, fully employed, and executive MBA students, all with at least four years work experience who expect a focus on current management issues throughout their studies. They enter the program with a real-world approach that shapes their expectation for just-in-time information. While we want our community of learners to understand that "learning to fish" for information is valuable, they want others to "fish for them." Meeting their expectations and educating them to the value of information literacy requires high profile and innovative approaches.

SEAMLESS SUPPORT IS A CRUCIAL INGREDIENT

Anderson Computing and Information Services (ACIS) provides integrated information, library and technology services to the UCLA Anderson School community. The Rosenfeld Library, the management library at UCLA, is part of ACIS as a result of a successful 1996 convergence of library and computing services (Frand & Bellanti, 1999). ACIS is a collaborative environment of library and computing professionals uniquely poised to design new products and services unencumbered by the traditional boundaries of libraries and computing centers. In the ACIS environment, librarians, computer support technicians, and programmers sit in cubicles side-by-side, and are involved in collaborative projects to improve our clients' abilities to access, gather, and manage the information they need. Teams investigate technological solutions that help students, faculty and staff work more effectively and efficiently.

VALUE PROPOSITION

ACIS has a long tradition of innovative products and services designed for graduate students. A needs-centered focus is a hallmark of our support. This approach has evolved over many years and enables us to identify support opportunities that have resulted in successful long-term relationships with several school programs and key stakeholders.

One such long-term relationship is with the program office that manages the MBA thesis-equivalent field study projects.[1] This office was undergoing an executive review in 1980 and was actively looking to enhance the student project experience. The library met this opportunity with a proposal for a team consultation service analogous to the services provided by corporate information centers at major accounting firms. Over the years, a majority of teams have made use of this voluntary service and it has become an integral part of field study projects, as well as a flagship offering of the library.

RESEARCH STRATEGIES, NOT ANSWERS

Our early instructional activities included a wide range of library- and technology-oriented workshops, delivered in traditional classroom style. Librarians provided the then typical one-hour guest lectures featuring show-and-tell of library sources as well as workshops covering specific assignment topics such as Sources for Accounting Standards. Computer technicians provided training on how to use the technology, including the major personal productivity packages such as Word, Excel and Power Point. In the early years, the technology workshops were mandatory, but over time, as these personal productivity packages moved into the workplace and undergraduate (and high school) programs, these workshops became voluntary and now are offered only to very small audiences.

A major conceptual breakthrough for our workshop approach occurred in the late 1980s when we conducted a session on locating statistics. This workshop was tied to a specific class assignment and focused on delivering research strategies for identifying and locating the best statistical data for the students' needs rather than on the usual show-and-tell of what library sources were physically available. The workshop was a huge success and taught us that our users were willing to accept research strategies in lieu of specific ready-reference type answers. It also reinforced how important faculty support in the form of a specific assignment is to students' motivation and commitment.

The switch to teaching research strategies instead of how-to-use tutorials meant a new relationship with our users and an opportunity to impart information seeking skills. In these earliest instances we provided the user with a view into the research process from the librarian's perspective, sharing the way we process a request and helping them understand what would spell research success. Figure 1, from the Locating Statistics Workshop, illustrates the technique of phrasing a request for data so that it gets the desired information as well as helping the user understand that data has characteristics.

JUST-IN-TIME

A decade later, during the late 1990s, another development spurred us in new directions. Stiff competition for the students' time outside the classroom combined with their ability to access information remotely saw attendance decline for our stand-alone workshops. What we started

FIGURE 1

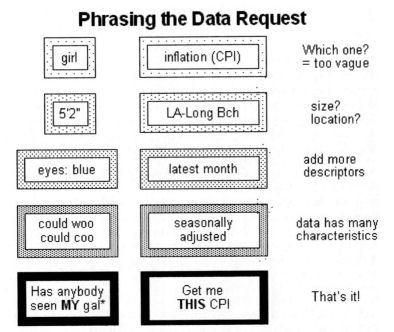

To Get What You Want,
State Fully What You Need.

*Music: Percy Wenrich / Lyrics: Jack Mahoney - 1914

to see was more focus on solutions for the immediate need and less concern for preparations for prospective information needs; or just-in-time instead of just-in-case. This was a reflection of an entire set of changes in students described in "The Information Age Mindset" (Frand, 2000).

Our involvement in the thesis-equivalent field study projects illustrates our just-in-time approach. These two-term projects coupled a team of three to five students with a participating company in a real-world problem-solving experience. Each team is offered one-hour consultations with two librarians at the crucial launching of the project. The librarians do not provide any research, but focus on providing a customized research strategy for the specific project. These sessions have proven to be extremely valuable to the teams, and program admin-

istrators have been moving to make the current online form of the
workshop required of all teams.

AN EARLY LIFE CYCLE APPROACH

In the 1980s we created a new master plan for the provision of all
our services based on what we called The Life Cycle of the MBA
Student (Figure 2). This planning tool identified the key events during the two years, from orientation week to graduation, that students
encounter while pursuing the MBA degree. We evaluated each event
in terms of potential library or computing support and linked them to
our existing services, programs, and other resources. This chart of
student needs along their MBA education timeline was then used to
identify new products and services that could be aligned in a
just-in-time fashion.

OUR OWN BRAND OF DIGITAL REFERENCE

Over the years, other facets of our services were re-cast with the
just-in-time approach. When reference desk use was plummeting across
the country, our own brand of virtual reference, eLibrarian (http://www.
anderson.ucla.edu/x15293.xml) offered research strategies instead of
ready reference answers (Borah, 2001). The response from our students
has been a steady and at times overwhelming demand for this online reference service. The life long benefit of the information literacy skills
provided within these research strategies is not lost on our students, as
evident in this recent comment from our user satisfaction survey: "It not
only directly helped with my MBA education but it also taught me some
research strategies which I will be able to carry with me in my future
career."

LIFE CYCLE GOES LIFELONG

To assure success in our plans for information literacy and other initiatives, we must focus on keeping content relevant by aligning it with
the user's own needs over the MBA student life cycle. However, recognizing that the MBA experience is just one part of the overall student
lifelong work future requires us to extend our thinking to meaningfully

FIGURE 2

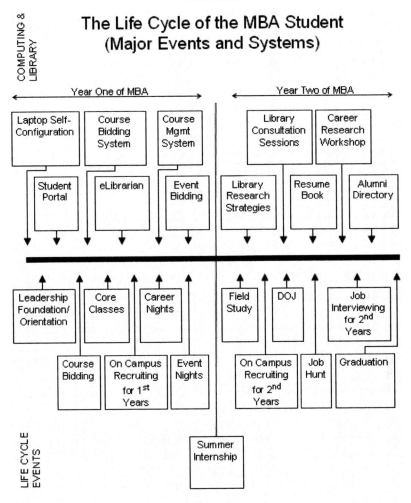

A concept created by Eloisa Yeargain and Marsha Smith in the 1980s, recreated from memory by Eloisa Borah, 3/17/2005

Life cycle events updated by Eric Mokover and Susan Corley, June 1, 2006

integrate information literacy instruction and services into the MBA experience, and also enables us to remain user-centered and ensure these efforts are aligned with post-MBA life needs. To assist with this effort, we have recently incorporated into our planning a new planning tool, Life Cycle of Business Information Needs (Figure 3), which maps business information needs over a lifetime of key decision points.

INFORMATION LITERACY CAMPAIGN

Information literacy gained traction at UCLA in 2001 when it was identified as a key strategic direction for the UCLA library system. These early efforts were focused on information competencies for undergraduate students (Caravello, Borah, Herschman, & Mitchell, 2001). ACIS saw a clear need to focus attention and resources on information literacy for graduate business students. With this in mind, ACIS launched the Information Literacy Campaign (ILC) in October 2002. We already had a great deal of success in a variety of library instructional offerings; however, the strength of the information literacy concept and the programmatic appeal of information literacy promised to help us move closer to a full integration with the MBA life cycle. With full integration we can achieve our vision of a holistic and integrated instructional program for our community of learners.

In keeping with our organizational structure, the ILC drew upon the insight and expertise of ACIS's diverse composition, forming a multi-functional team of librarians, technology support staff, software programmers, and Web developers to work on the project. The ILC was charged to investigate information literacy for MBA students; propose an "information literacy" definition appropriate for graduate management students; conduct an assessment of current Anderson MBA student information and technology competencies; and recommend next steps for information literacy at the UCLA Anderson School of Management.

DEFINING INFORMATION LITERACY

The ILC began its work by considering various definitions of information literacy before arriving at its own definition. A number of considerations informed the ILC definition. As a graduate level program, the definition had to emphasize higher order cognitive skills, such as

FIGURE 3

Life Cycle
of Business Information Needs

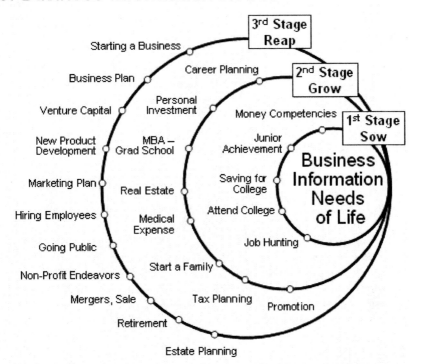

critical thinking for problem solving and decision making. As a professional program, an outward focus on professional workplace skills and lifelong learning was essential. In addition, we subscribed to a broad view of information literacy that encompassed competencies in both information and technology. Our unique organizational perspective as a combined library and technology organization played a role in taking this broad view, as did our practical experience, which told us that information and technology are so deeply linked from a student's perspective that we could not and should not treat them separately. This perspective also represents an alignment with the goals for the UCLA Anderson MBA programs, which foster:

- A sophisticated awareness of the global, technological, and competitive forces shaping business.
- Analytical problem-solving skills that directly relate to critical business issues.
- A high-level ability to exercise sound judgment, make effective decisions, and take appropriate responsibility.
- Strong interpersonal, communication, teamwork, and leadership skills.
- A strategic understanding of the role of information and communication technologies in business and management (UCLA Anderson School of Management, 2006).

With these considerations in mind, the taskforce arrived at a definition of information literacy,[2] branded InfoIQ, which embodied these ideas. InfoIQ is conceptual and technological abilities to find, retrieve, evaluate and use business information for effective and efficient decision-making and problem solving in furtherance of professional and organizational goals. Recently, we have evolved a simpler marketing-oriented definition: Management success = IQ + Emotional IQ + InfoIQ, where IQ refers to the knowledge gained through the MBA curriculum, Emotional IQ refers to the people skills needed, and InfoIQ represents the information and technology competency dimension.

MBA INFORMATION LITERACY ASSESSMENT

The taskforce next undertook an extensive review to identify existing information literacy benchmarks for MBA students. A likely source, the Association to Advance Collegiate Schools of Business (AACSB), the accrediting agency for degree programs in business administration and accounting, does not discuss nor provide benchmarks for business information literacy at this time (Advance Collegiate Schools of Business, 2006). In the absence of existing standards, the taskforce conducted an initial assessment to gain a snapshot of student attitudes towards information and technology and to gain an understanding of skill levels. The informal assessment consisted of focus groups conducted with current students in the three MBA programs and recent alumni. Focus group findings fell into seven areas or attitudes about information and technology (Figure 4).

INFOIQ COMPETENCIES

In the absence of information literacy competencies for graduate business students, the ILC drafted competencies to serve as a framework for MBA student assessment. Figure 5 outlines eleven competencies and eleven performance indicators. The indicators serve as guidelines for faculty (or any assessor) to assess a student in that competency area. Given the difficulty of assessing student competencies, these have not yet been tested at the time this article was written. They have, however, guided us in the development of InfoIQ instructional content.

INFOIQ TRANSITION

UCLA Anderson MBA programs seek to transform students into business leaders "able to identify new opportunities, adapt quickly to unpredictable conditions and work with diverse groups of people (UCLA Anderson School of Management, 2006). The transformation from MBA student to business professional requires a significant change in attitude and thinking about today's complex information and technology environment. Figure 6 illustrates the characteristics of this transition from a student perspective of information that it is ubiquitous, cheap, instantaneous, and automatic to a professional perspective of information that it is ambiguous, requiring skill, incomplete, complex, and expensive.[3] The role of the faculty and librarians in this transition is to develop learning models and programs that test student assumptions in a manner that helps them make this transition.

INFOIQ PILOT PROGRAM

As a result of the ILC findings, ACIS launched a one-year InfoIQ pilot program in summer 2005 to develop and deliver services related to the effective student use of information, communication, and technology tools and resources (Lippincott & Kuchida, 2005). Three goals were established for the pilot. First, from an organizational standpoint, the pilot program would serve as a proof of concept for the MBA program administrators and faculty stakeholders. Importantly the pilot would integrate new and existing services and activities under the

FIGURE 4

Needs Assessment focus group findings	
"I'm OK, but you're not"	• High confidence in own ability to find information. • Low opinion of others' skills. • High technical skill does not guarantee good information, but low technical skill certainly was a hindrance.
It's the tools	• Tools are an obstacle to finding good information. • Tools are not smart enough. • Certain tools difficult to use. • Constant change of technology an obstacle.
Technical skills = information literacy	• High technical skill equals high information literacy. • However, low technical skill does not equal low information literacy.
Information independence	• Information independence is a term that means varying things to different people. • Some find independence by taking classes, learning tools, doing it themselves and becoming experts. • Others equate independence with finding an expert, one who may not necessarily teach a skill but uses their skill to help a non-expert.
Go with what you've got	• Good information is not necessarily the best or most relevant information but what you can find with the time given. • Go with the first search "hits."
Too much information	• There is often too much information. • Difficult to decipher what is good or useful. • More information leads to more complexity and more ambiguity. • Expectation to find good data is higher because data appears to be more accessible and abundant.
Minimum technical competencies	• It is important to have minimum technical competency. • Disagreement about how minimum technical competency is defined • It depends on the environment - one size does not fit all.

InfoIQ brand. Second, the pilot program would help ACIS further develop its InfoIQ vision which emphasized a unified approach that would bring together diverse departments and stakeholders to form partnerships. The third goal was instructionally oriented: to address several of the factors influencing the need for information and technology instruction programs for MBA students, many of which surfaced during the ILC assessment focus groups. These included the "access paradox" (Borah, Kuchida, Lippincott, Lee, & Rajaran, 2004), the growing gap between student skills and access to the vast information and technol-

FIGURE 5

Competency	Indicator
1.1 Able to recognize and articulate an information or technology need exists for a given task. [*Identify*]	1.2 Displays a method of initial analysis or assessment of technology or of information resources for a task.
2.1 Able to identify information and technology resources for a particular industry, organization, or task. [*Identify*]	2.2 Displays the ability to use the appropriate channels to locate information sources and technology available or commonly used in a particular environment for a task
3.1 Able to access needed information and technology effectively and efficiently. [*Retrieve*]	3.1 Selects options wisely to formulate search statements resulting in on-target, cost-analyzed information retrieval, and refines search strategies when necessary.
4.1 Able to analyze/evaluate costs versus benefits (time, price, convenience, etc) of selecting and using various information/technology resources. [*Evaluate*]	4.1 Demonstrates understanding of free versus for-fee resources and the potential trade-offs associated with each.
5.1 Able to evaluate data retrieved on the basis of factors such as credibility, relevance, novelty, and comprehensiveness. [*Evaluate*]	5.2 Exhibits awareness of the need to evaluate data based on source and other factors. Accepts or rejects data based on evaluation.
6.1 Able to utilize information to solve problems and make decisions. [*Utilize*]	6.2 Demonstrates ability to manipulate data/information or make use of available information to make decisions.
7.1 Able to organize and manage information. [*Utilize*]	7.2 Demonstrates ability to sort the information gathered, identify and note key points.
8.1 Able to adopt and adapt to technology and information resources used by an organization or business. [*Utilize*]	8.2 Demonstrates ability to learn and be familiar with current information and technology resources.
9.1 Able to determine when the solution is to go with something entirely new. [*Create*]	9.2 Demonstrates ability to plot a course of action to determine when a solution is not among the existing cost-effective options.
10.1 Able to design new information options. [*Create*]	10.2 Demonstrates ability to assess information and technology skills and resources for new needs.
11.1 Able to recognize broader use of information at hand. [*Create*]	11.2 Demonstrates ability to spot the multi-discipline, multi-application of information.

FIGURE 6

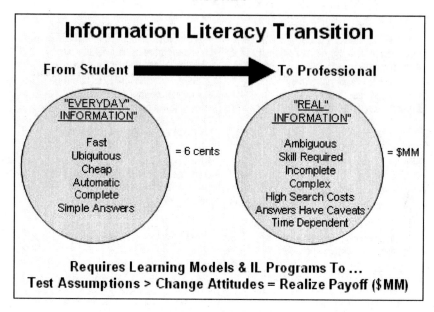

ogy resources available to them, and the related concept of information overload (too much complex information, too widely dispersed), as well as the changing expectations of students suggested by the "It's the tools" attitude displayed by focus group participants (Figure 4).

IDENTIFYING A PILOT PARTNER

The taskforce selected the field study program as the most appropriate to target for the InfoIQ pilot. As discussed earlier, the field study course is a two-quarter master's thesis project that employs experiential learning whereby teams partner with a company to work on a business objective identified by that company. Overseen by a faculty advisor, teams identify and analyze the business problem, conduct primary and secondary research, and present a strategy or solution to the company. Companies pay a fee to participate in this project.[4]

The field study program represented the best fit for information and technology literacy efforts for a number of reasons. The library had an on-going relationship with this program office. The overall aim of the project is to integrate student learning in the core academic areas through active application. In addition to integrating core business and management concepts, students develop skills in project scoping and management, client management, teamwork, communication, primary research, and secondary research. The curricular approach of the project aligned perfectly with our goal of reaching beyond the classroom. Unlike the more highly structured case and lecture-based course curriculum, the field study experience is build upon a real world situation where students are required to gather and analyze complex information to solve an unstructured business problem. Students are likely to face similar challenges throughout their careers, increasing the opportunity for InfoIQ skill transfer. We already witness such transfers as our students return after graduation to do research in the library, with our field study research strategy handout in hand. Finally, student motivation, an important ingredient of successful learning, is high because the project has real outcomes. High stakeholder expectations mean that the pressure to perform and the consequences of failure are real to the student and the company.

FROM SUPPORT TO PARTNERSHIP

The InfoIQ team recognized that a pilot with the field study program required an expansion of the relationship between ACIS and the field study office from one of providing ancillary support services to one of partnership with full integration of InfoIQ into the field study curriculum. Consequently, the team undertook a detailed analysis of the field study program to determine how we could build upon our current relationship. We investigated how current services to the field study program met their needs and where the InfoIQ program could add greater value to student learning. Working with the field study program director, the InfoIQ team identified several instructional content areas key for student success in the field study program, including project scoping, client management, primary research, communication, teamwork, collaboration in virtual environments (teamwork, information creation and sharing, and communication), secondary business research (strategies, sources, search techniques, and citing sources), and personal knowledge management (organize, store, find, and retrieve personal information).

ONLINE DELIVERY

It became apparent that the field study program faced many of the same challenges that we faced in terms of finding ways to integrate instruction into the field study curriculum. The field study project was designed so that a team's work was supervised by a faculty advisor. This approach, as opposed to a field study course that all students would attend, allowed for wide variations in how teams carried out the field study project based on preferences of the field study faculty advisor.[5] In the absence of a parallel course, it was difficult to integrate instruction into the project. To overcome this barrier, the InfoIQ team concentrated on online delivery of instructional content, developing an interactive workshop, "Smart Strategies for Business Research." The design of the workshop was modular, consisting of a four-part strategy for secondary field study research aligned with the MBA competencies (Figure 4): identify (define), retrieve, evaluate (refine), utilize (use), and create. By employing the "strategies, not answers" approach, we sought to demonstrate the value of the strategy as a roadmap to research beyond the field study project. The workshop also represented a further refinement of the just-in-time approach discussed earlier. Students could take the workshop online at their convenience and could return to review a module at any time during the project.

About half of the field study teams were required to complete the workshop early in the project and use it to prepare their initial project planning documents. Extremely positive feedback from students indicated the workshop was very valuable to them. These comments sum up the general sentiment from students[6]:

> "This workshop is invaluable! My only wish is that I could have taken this workshop prior to starting the FEMBA program. The quality of my projects would certainly have been enhanced had it been exposed to this workshop 2 years ago. This one workshop has minimized if not eliminated the burden associated with learning how to do secondary research."

> "One very useful part of the workshop is to provide a step by step research plan. Now, I can define, identify, use, evaluate and refine the vast online information available. I can also follow the provided search steps which are: Company and Competitive Picture–Industry–Market–Country."

Feedback from the program administrator and faculty advisors indicated that they felt the overall quality of the project planning at the early stages was improved. The major factors contributing to the success of the project were the just-in-time approach, online delivery, self-paced format, interactivity, multimedia integration, the use of quizzes and exercises to reinforce content, and emphasis on transferable strategies (Lippincott & Oppenheim, 2006). The secondary research online workshop required in conjunction with the library's team consultation service proved to be a powerful approach indeed.

INSTRUCTIONAL TECHNOLOGY AND DESIGN

The success of this workshop resulted in an important new role for the InfoIQ program in developing and delivering a suite of online instructional modules that encompasses the range of soft skills needed to successfully complete the field study project. This represents a substantial step in bringing the InfoIQ program closer to its goal of curricular integration. It became clear that this was the path to moving our program from service provision to partnership. We realized that our success was not only in differentiating our products and services under the InfoIQ brand, but recognizing that InfoIQ is part of a larger set of interrelated skills. The InfoIQ program could play an important role in promoting the entire range of skills while emphasizing the importance of information and technology skills. The InfoIQ team began working with content experts to develop online workshops on project scoping and primary research, two of the instructional content areas identified by the field study director and InfoIQ team. With these projects underway, we have clearly moved closer to partnership with the field study program.

At the same time, the InfoIQ team began sponsoring collaboration and instructional technology pilots, rolling out to student teams SAKAI (online collaboration and learning environment software to support team and course work), Microsoft SharePoint (collaboration and document management), and Adobe Breeze (Web conferencing and real-time collaboration) tools and associated training in effective virtual team collaboration. The role of ACIS is to investigate and implement technology solutions for effective and efficient work so this was a natural fit for the InfoIQ pilot. This did, however, represent an expansion of the notion of InfoIQ from teaching effective use of information and technology to providing technology solutions.

WHAT LIES AHEAD

The InfoIQ pilot ended in September 2006 with a great deal of progress made, but also much work ahead. In terms of the three InfoIQ pilot goals, we made substantial gains in proving the worth of InfoIQ to program administrators, we integrated new services and products under the InfoIQ brand, and we reached a majority of the MBA students with an initial InfoIQ instructional module. An assessment of the one-year pilot will focus on determining reach and impact of instructional content and collaborative pilot projects.

In addition to completing the primary research and project scoping instructional modules, two major focuses for the future are collaboration (local and remote team work) and personal knowledge management. Learning to work effectively as a member of a decision- and information-focused team and leveraging available communication and collaboration technologies are critical for effective leaders of the 21st century. We will continue to pilot instructional and collaboration technologies that move us forward in this area.

Attitudes are changing, partnerships have been strengthened or formed, and through our InfoIQ effort ACIS is well positioned to advocate for information and technology literacy as a critical component of the entire Anderson experience. ACIS has taken the long view and our MBA students will reap the benefits for a lifetime.

NOTES

1. This is a two-quarter team consultation with a company. There are approximately 100 teams each year with three to five students per team. About half the companies are U.S.-based and the remaining are from dozens of countries around the world.

2. Our work was informed by definitions from the National Forum on Information Literacy (http://www.infolit.org/definitions.html, accessed on April 20, 2005) and Association of College and Research Libraries. (http://www.ala.org/ala/acrl/acrlissues/acrlinfolit/informationliteracy.htm/, accessed on April 20, 2005).

3. This diagram resulted from a discussion between author, Aura Lippincott and Dr. Robert S. Spich, Senior Lecturer, Management and International Business, UCLA Anderson School of Management.

4. During the 2005-2006 academic year, there were 126 teams working with companies scattered across five countries located on three continents.

5. As of this writing, the school has implemented a parallel course for one of its three MBA degree programs.

6. We received 150 comments from 36 field study teams. Of these, 148 were positive.

REFERENCES

Advance Collegiate Schools of Business. (2006). *Eligibility procedures and accreditation standards for business accreditation.* http://www.aacsb.edu/accreditation/business/STANDARDS.pdf.

Borah, E. G. (2001). *eLibrarian: It's not your father's e-mail reference.* Proceedings of the 3rd Annual Virtual Reference Desk Conference. Orlando, FL, November 12-13, 2001. Retrieved August 10, 2006, from http://www.vrd.org/conferences/VRD2001/proceedings/borah.shtml.

Borah, E., Kuchida, H., Lippincott, A., Lee, D., & Rajaran, S. (2004). *Access paradox: An information literacy campaign response.* Presented at the eLit 2004 Conference, June 1-3, 2004. Retrieved August 10, 2006, from http://elit-conf.org/elit2004/parallelsessions.html#session3.

Caravello, P. S., Borah, E. G., Herschman, J., & Mitchell, E. (2001). *Information competence at UCLA: Report of a survey project.* Los Angeles, CA: UCLA Library. Information Literacy. Retrieved August 10, 2006, from http://repositories.cdlib.org/uclalib/il/01.Frand, J. (2000, September/October). The information-age mindset: Changes in students and implications for higher education. *Educause Review, 35.*

Frand, J. (2000, September/October). The information-age mindset: Changes in students and implications for higher education. *Educause Review, 35.*

Frand, J., & Bellanti, B. (1999, October 7). *Collaborative convergence: Merging computing and library services at the Anderson Graduate School of Management at UCLA.* (Working article). http://www.anderson.ucla.edu/faculty/jason.frand/researcher/articles/ComputerLibraryIntegration.htm. (Published in the *Journal of Business & Finance Librarianship,* 6(2): 2000).

Lippincott, A., & Kuchida, H. (2005, August 1). InfoIQ: A service offering of UCLA Anderson Computing and Information Services. *Anderson Graduate School of Management. Information and Technology. article InfoIQ.* Retrieved August 10, 2006, from http://repositories.cdlib.org/anderson/IandT/InfoIQ.

Lippincott, A., & Oppenheim, M. (2006). *Rapid eLearning with Articulate Presenter and Adobe/Macromedia Captivate.* Presented to the Special Libraries Association San Diego Chapter, October 6, 2006. Retrieved August 10, 2006, from http://slasd.pbwiki.com/auralippincott.

UCLA Anderson School of Management. (n.d.) *The learning model.* Retrieved August 8, 2006, from http://www.anderson.ucla.edu/x2965.xml.

UCLA Anderson School of Management. (n.d.) *Discover the Anderson advantage.* Retrieved August 10, 2006, from http://www.anderson.ucla.edu/x47.xml.

A Library Research Course for Graduate and Professional Students in Communication Sciences and Disorders

Sylvia G. Tag

INTRODUCTION

Western Washington University (WWU) is a state institution with a student population of approximately 12,000. WWU distinguishes itself from the larger Ph.D. granting institutions in Washington State by its emphasis on undergraduate education services. Although the primary focus is undergraduate education, WWU offers select graduate programs at the master's level through the College of Humanities and Social Sciences, the College of Education, the College of Business and Economics, and the Huxley School of the Environment. Individual departments on campus may offer a master's degree program, for example, the History Department's program of Archives and Records Management and the English Department's master's programs in English Studies and Creative Writing. Other departments may offer master's degree programs to small numbers of students.

The department of Communication Sciences and Disorders (CSD) offers a two-year Master of Arts degree in Speech-language Pathology. The department consists of six full time faculty and eight full/part-time clinical educators. Admission to the program is highly competitive with approximately 20 students admitted annually. The CSD department is accredited by the American Speech-Language Hearing Association's Council on Academic Accreditation in Audiology and Speech-Language Pathology (CAA), The Northwest Commission on Colleges and Universities (NWCCU), and by the National Council for the Accreditation of Teacher Education (NCATE).

In addition to the academic department, an on-site speech-language-hearing clinic provides services to the community. Through practicum studies, students work with clients while under the direct supervision of clinical educators and department faculty. As stated in the Western Washington University Bulletin (2006-2007), "Faculty and professional staff at the CSD department have a responsibility for the welfare of patients tested, treated, or otherwise affected by students enrolled in the CSD program. The department has the ultimate responsibility to the public to assure its graduates can become fully competent audiologists and speech-language pathologists, capable of delivering quality care in a timely manner and preserving the well-being of the patients they serve. Thus it is important that persons admitted, retained and graduated possess the intelligence, integrity, compassion, humanitarian concern, and physical and emotional capacity necessary to practice speech-language pathology and audiology." This eloquent statement reflects the commitment of the CSD department faculty and clinical staff towards a comprehensive education for their students at the undergraduate and graduate level. The department mission statement is included in Appendix A.

In 2003, the library initiated a proposal to provide a course on research skills to graduate students in the CSD program. The library credit class described in this article was developed to provide research strategies, skills, and competencies as CSD students begin their graduate studies as well as to prepare students to advance their own continuing education. The initial idea for a credit course, the evolution of the syllabus, the sustainability requirements, and future goals are discussed.

LITERATURE REVIEW

Library and information science literature includes articles that examine and recommend resources and collections related to CSD, but there is no specific mention of instruction services. A review of the literature in the field of communication sciences and disorders yields similar results for library services. This does not mean that there is a complete lack of interaction between libraries and the field of CSD. Rather, issues related to research strategies are found in the discussion of information access for the health sciences and health care providers. In fact, there is a tremendous amount of popular and academic literature on information-seeking strategies in the health sciences. One of the best examples is *Educational Services in Health Sciences Libraries* edited by Alison Bunting (1995). Covering a breadth of instruction opportunities, this book includes techniques for providing classroom instruction as well as developing a comprehensive program in conjunction with a hospital or large research institution. Written at the beginning of the explosion of Internet resources and interfaces, the authors anticipated the continuing role of librarians as educators.

And how are librarians doing as educators? A recent questionnaire distributed to molecular biology graduate students at the University of Oklahoma reveals that the majority of students go directly to e-journal subscriptions and online medical resources like PubMed when they are searching for journal literature. Students totally bypass the library and proprietary databases (Brown, 2005). While no doubt effective, students who limit their findings to readily available research literature are missing a wealth of relevant information. The power of the Internet and the phenomenon of end-user searching have not diminished the objectives of locating and using discipline specific materials, but the spectrum of resources is changing the research process in profound ways. A project at the London Health Libraries identified three important teaching traits for effective library instruction: professional competency, teaching skills, and e-learning skills. Within these categories, personal information literacy, understanding of popular applications, fluency with relevant information systems and fluency with various learning environments stand out as especially important (Robinson et al., 2005).

There are ongoing instruction efforts in health science libraries, hospitals, and clinics. A comprehensive collection of articles about instruction services is found in *A Guide to Developing End User Education Programs in Medical Libraries*, edited by Elizabeth Connor (2005). Contributors describe programs at hospitals and research institutions. Faculty-librarian collaboration, e-learning, curriculum integration and outreach are included. Most chapters include examples of assignments, handouts, and assessments.

Occasional articles in health sciences and library literature include examples of library instruction services to graduate students. A library course on electronic resources for the life sciences is taught at the University of Illinois at Urbana-Champaign. The library was approached by a faculty member in the biology department and the course was created collaboratively. The author states that "one positive outcome of offering a formal course in library instruction has been the increased visibility of the library as a key information resource, rather than merely a place where fewer and fewer journals are stored" (Schmidt, 1993, p. 57). The availability of online teaching tools can provide a practical means for teaching large numbers of students. A successful graduate course at Wayne State University uses Blackboard courseware to teach research skills (Bhavnagri & Bielat, 2005). The Graduate School of Management and Technology at the University of Maryland offers a Web-based course. Designed collaboratively, the course is fee-based, required, and non-credit (Kelley, Orr, Houck, & Weber, 2001).

Applied ethics regarding intellectual property is discussed regularly in higher education, with particular attention to plagiarism. Academic dishonesty in graduate school is especially egregious because the student is becoming a part of a professional community. In her article on combating plagiarism, Hamilton encourages librarians to be part of the solution by learning about plagiarism detection tools and sharing these with faculty (2003). However, this is only part of the solution. Libraries must respond by developing relevant and practical instruction services that provide a rationale for ethical research rather than relying solely on punitive threats. As noted by Woolf et al. (2005), the health care system as a whole does not do an adequate job of responding to the growing need for health information on the Internet. In response, leading academic universities (e.g., Berkeley, Yale, Michigan) have developed Web sites on public health information (Larson, 1999). Even public libraries are using data from the 2003 National Survey of Student Engagement (NSSE), Laird reports that the overall impact of technology on student education is positive, especially in terms of collaborative learning and student-faculty interactions (2004). However, using technology is different than the effective and efficient extraction of research materials. For example, it is essential to know the difference between *Healthfinder.gov*, a good resource for patients, *PubMed*, an online resource published by the National Institutes of Health that provides free abstracts and fee-based full text, and *Medline*, a part of PubMed that is available through a proprietary database vendor.

In the health sciences, two important higher education pedagogies have emerged. Problem-based learning (PBL) is a curricular approach that is learner-driven and collaborative and may be used for discussing and solving practical issues. A familiar library PBL application is a credible literature review as part of a term article or project. Evidence-based learning (EBL) integrates personal expertise with the best available information from systematic research. As part of a patient-centered practice, the gathering of evidence (research) on the part of the practitioner and the client is commonplace (Hendler, 2004). CSD graduate students at WWU work in the campus Speech and Hearing Clinic. Therefore, in addition to their own coursework, students may be in the role of educating patients. Both of these pedagogies are a part of the CSD program at WWU and are integrated into library instruction. As information formats, interfaces, and access issues continue to evolve, information-seeking competencies are more important than ever before and it is from this perspective that the CSD graduate course was developed and is sustained.

DEVELOPMENT OF THE GRADUATE COURSE

Articulating the Instruction Need

A credit course for students in the CSD program was created as a result of student feedback, faculty observation, and assessment data. Prior to the development of a credit course, students received library instruction in a traditional bibliographic instruction setting. In an effort to apply effective teaching strategies, the instruction sessions were course-integrated, students had papers and assignments that utilized library resources, and communication between the department faculty and the library was excellent. However, even with these important components in place, observations and conversations indicated that the one-shot bibliographic instruction teaching model was not optimally suited to this student population.

During the 2002 academic year, instruction evaluations were given to four CSD courses–three undergraduate and one graduate. Results from the undergraduate students revealed that approximately half the students received some kind of library instruction. Retention and practical application was inconsistent and varied widely depending on when the library instruction was provided. Graduate students appreciated the sessions and made particular suggestions, going as far as requesting extended instruction and linking library instruction to specific courses. (See Appendix B.)

The library instruction evaluations provided a springboard for discussions between department faculty and the library. A library proposal was presented to the entire CSD faculty and staff in the spring of 2003. (See Appendix C.) The discussion centered on the content, length and grading aspects of the course. It was agreed that the first effort should be a trial. Library sessions would take place over five evenings during fall quarter for the graduate students and five evenings during winter quarter for undergraduates. Attendance was optional but highly encouraged.

The Instruction Trial

Standardized university assessment forms were distributed to the students who attended the sessions. The form asked 20 questions on course content and instructor effectiveness on a ranked scale of 0-5. The student response distribution varied from 3.61 to 4.78, which is in the very good to excellent range. Some students found the first sessions were a review while others were grateful for the orientation to library. Most of the feedback centered on the value of pertinent, connected resources. Monday evenings seemed to be a difficult time for the class due to jobs, family, and the rigor of the CSD program. From the instructor's perspective, content continuity and work expectations were marginalized because there was no required component.

A meeting to review the trial classes took place in the summer of 2004. There was a general consensus to require completion for all entering graduate students. The CSD program is demanding and in order to minimize the impact the course was set at one-credit with a satisfactory/unsatisfactory grading scale. The class was moved from Monday evenings to Thursday mornings to integrate the course into the weekly schedule. A second significant decision was to list the course under the CSD department. Sustained by the department, the course is not tied to a particular librarian but is integrated into the curriculum. In the fall of 2004 the class was taught for credit and required for all newly admitted graduate students.

DEPARTMENT INTEGRATION

The CSD department has developed undergraduate and graduate learning goals based on the certification standards established by the American Speech-Language-Hearing Association. Specific course-related learning objectives link to overarching goals or "standards." The library graduate course, CSD 589, links to Standard III-F (American Speech-Language-Hearing Association, 2005).

Standard III-F: The student must demonstrate knowledge of processes used in research, including the use of information technology. Implementation by the Western Washington University CSD Department:

> The student must demonstrate information literacy by demonstrating knowledge of the social aspects of information, the organization of information, and the research process. This information will be obtained through a course, "Library Strategies for CSD," and through applied practice in departmental writing proficiency courses. Information also may be obtained through class projects, clinical experiences, independent studies, and research projects.

Library instruction is part of the department's evidence for American Speech-Language-Hearing Association accreditation. At the undergraduate level, *LIBR403: Research Tutorial for CSD* is offered. While taking this library course, students may apply their learning to concurrent CSD courses. In fact, *CSD373: Introduction to Phonology* requires a linked assignment. At the graduate level, students take *CSD589:Research for CSD* during their initial fall quarter so that they are better equipped for using information technology as they complete projects associated with graduate courses over the next six quarters.

COURSE DESCRIPTION

Goals and Objectives

Course objectives are taken from the Western Libraries Instruction Program and then customized for the discipline of CSD (Western Washington University, 2006). The library class has three overarching goals, each of which contains a varying number of underlying learning objectives: the social aspect of information, the organization of information, and the research process.

The social aspect of information is best characterized by the phrase *Teach the Teacher*. A master's degree in CSD is a terminal degree and after students graduate they will be the educators of clients and patients. This will take place in an ever-changing health care environment. As future clinicians, students will probably not be teaching their patients how to do research per se. However, they will need to model the ethics of information retrieval by knowing the sources of their own knowledge. In addition, all citizens should formulate opinions on censorship, intellectual freedom, and respect for differing points of view. Finally, as health care providers, there will be opportunities to inform clients regarding online searching and authoritative Internet resources. Current characteristics of the provider-patient climate include:

- The general population is mobile. There are very few family physicians that follow patients through their lives. We are keepers of our own health care information.
- Managed care plans and insurance policies influence treatment options and choices.
- There is an ownership of fitness in our society which manifests itself in patient activism and second opinions.
- Medicine is constantly in the news/media: biotechnology, genetics, infomercials, etc.
- Consumers have a "get it now" attitude–millions of people seek health care advice online
- Online health sites are popular because consumers can be anonymous: online resources don't "judge" or give anyone a "funny look."
- Even savvy Internet users can succumb to information overload: if it looks familiar, we trust it. So, the first Web page that resonates is used.

- Many sites have disclaimers that say "consult your physician" but people don't always do this. The obvious example is drugs that can react differently in different people.

The organization of information is another focus of the course. Students are asked to demonstrate knowledge of scholarly, trade, and popular publications in the field of communication sciences and disorders. Particular questions include:

- What is the importance of research data in this field? Who is talking to whom?
- How does citation behavior function in the CSD scholarly community?
- Students should be able to explain the difference between controlled/subject vocabulary and free text. For example, the medical subject headings, MeSH, are very relevant to CSD research.

The research process objectives are the most familiar to students. Plagiarism and intellectual property are discussed within the context of student research and client education. Particular questions and tasks include:

- Explain how search terms may vary with time and context
- Demonstrate a variety of search techniques
- Use the components of a citation to choose those most suitable for the information need, using criteria such as currency, reputation of the author or source, formats, elements of the URL, etc.
- Demonstrate the use of elements that help in analyzing the reliability of the information: table of contents, abstracts, bibliography, editorial review process, URL analysis, provenance and organization of the material
- Give examples of how conflicting opinions are negotiated within a discipline
- Recognize that information-seeking is an evolving, non-linear process that involves making a set of choices

Course Content

The syllabus, assignments, and course documents are all available online through Blackboard courseware. The communication features of Blackboard, particularly announcements and communication via e-mail, help to make the logistical management reasonable for a class that meets just once a week. Completion of all assignments is required to pass the course.

The first assignment asks students to examine the information environment for care providers and patients. To prompt their reflection, they read several articles on this topic. (See Appendix D.) The class discussion is usually interesting as students find out that there are a variety of search experiences in the classroom. Multiply this by hundreds and one can get a glimpse of the vast array of circumstances that they will be dealing with as practitioners. This assignment also serves as a means of reviewing citation skills.

The second assignment (see Appendix E) builds on the first by asking the students to create a brochure using the Microsoft Publisher program. The information may come from journals, books, government information, reference materials or the Web. The brochure is for patient education and so the terminology must either be defined or understandable by a non-professional. All images must be credited. Any text that is quoted or paraphrased must be cited. The brochure is shared with the Communication Sciences and Disorders faculty and clinical staff. Some of the brochures are selected for use in the campus speech and hearing clinic. This class session is taught by a guest instructor from the campus Student Technology Center.

The third assignment (Appendix F) is a demonstration of the student's skill at retrieving information from the variety of resources that are covered in class. Specialized databases for CSD, related subject databases in the disciplines of psychology, education, and medicine, and measurement tests and scales are all demonstrated. Government information is relevant to CSD, for example the Americans with Disabilities Act, PubMed and information published by the National Institutes of Health. By the end of the class, students should feel confident that they can shape a search with refined terminology, locate relevant information, adjust their search according to their search results and retrieve enough material to satisfy their own curiosity and the assignment parameters.

The final assignment (Appendix G) is a reflective essay. Graduate students are participants in the community of CSD scholars and practitioners. They are asked to articulate their understanding of how information functions within their chosen discipline.

CONCLUSION

The course described in this article took several years to develop into its current form and could not exist without input from students, faculty and the library. Taken at the beginning of their graduate program, the course is the start of a continuing relationship between the library and the student. Annual assessment reports, linked assignments, and occasional face-to-face meetings keep the department faculty informed regarding updates and changes to the course content. Finally, the predictable structure of an annual course aids in resource planning for the library.

For libraries that are considering offering credit courses to graduate students, the process described in this article offers several points to keep in mind. Assessment is the place to start. Ideas, anecdotes, and hunches about implementing instruction programs must be supported by data. Fact-gathering through assessment is critical in providing a rationale to department faculty. Graduate students describe themselves as busy and over-burdened. Ongoing feedback from students aids in content revision and keeps the focus of the course relevant and useful. From the library's perspective, assessment information is important, especially when considering the challenges we face in terms of student populations, library staffing levels, and work-load issues.

As mentioned in the Instruction Trial section of this article, this graduate course does not "count" within the university instruction system as a library course. The undergraduate course, mentioned briefly, has a library course number but the graduate course is taught through the CSD department. This means that the library cannot list the course in their annual report of instruction services. Individual institutions will need to review their instruction program guidelines to decide the practical and political ramifications if they find themselves in a similar situation.

Communication between the library and department faculty is key. After the initial trial, there was a thorough and candid review of what worked and what didn't. Faculty can promote and support the course to students and they may even learn about new library resources themselves through continuing dialog. Linked assignments that are co-graded provide a practical means of reinforcing the connection between the library and the department. This course benefits from the fact that there are national standards issued by the American Speech-Language-Hearing Association that incorporate the principles of information literacy instruction. Many disciplines have standards that address issues of information retrieval and research and these can provide a foundation for library instruction and lifelong learning.

The best illustration of the collaborative effort of this instruction project took place in 2004, the first year that the credit course was offered. The entire CSD faculty joined the class. Sitting in the front row, they took notes, participated in discussions and brought their expertise to the course. The faculty no longer attends, but their presence for the first official class was a generous affirmation that the work of developing the course was, and is, well worth the benefits.

REFERENCES

American Speech-Language-Hearing Association. (2005). Membership and certification handbook of the American Speech-Language-Hearing Association: For speech-language pathology. Retrieved June 11, 2007, from http://www.asha.org/about/membership-certification/handbooks/slp/slp_standards.htm.

Bhavnagri, N. P., & Bielat, V. (2005). Faculty-librarian collaboration to teach research skills: Electronic symbiosis. *Reference Librarian*, 89/90, 121-138.

Brown, C. (2005). Where do molecular biology graduate students find information? *Science and Technology Libraries*, 25, 89-104.

Bunting, A. (1995). *Educational services in health sciences libraries*. Metuchen, NJ.: Scarecrow Press.

Conner, E. (2005). *A guide to developing end user education programs in medical libraries*. New York: Haworth Press.

Hamilton, D. (2003). Plagiarism: Librarians help provide new solutions to an old problem. *Searcher, 11*(4), 26-28.

Hendler, G. Y. (2004). Why evidence-based medicine matters to patients. *Journal of Consumer Health on the Internet*, 8(2), 1-14.

Kelley, K. B., Orr, G. J., Houck, J., & SchWeber, C. (2001). Library instruction for the next millennium: Two Web-based courses to teach distant students information literacy. *Journal of Library Administration*, *32*, 281-294.

Laird, T. F. (2004). *Student experiences with information technology and their relationship to other aspects of student engagement*. Retrieved April 10, 2007 from Indiana University, National Survey of Student Engagement Web site: nsse.iub.edu/pdf/AIR2004EngagementWithITFinal.pdf.

Larson, C. A. (1999). Academic public health resources: A review of nine American Web pages. *Health Care on the Internet*, 3(4), 29-37.

Robinson, L., Hilger-Ellis, J., Osborne, L., Rowlands, J., Smith, J. M., West, A., Whetherly, J., et al. (2005). Healthcare librarians and learner support: A review of competencies and methods. *Health Information and Libraries Journal*, 22(Suppl. 2), 42-50.

Snyder, M., Huber, J.T., & Wegmann, D. (2002). Education for the consumer: A train the trainer collaboration. *Health Care on the Internet: A Journal of Methods & Applications*, 6(4), 49-62.

Western Washington University bulletin. (2006-2007). Bellingham, WA.: Western Washington University.

Western Washington University Libraries. (2006, Fall). *Western Washington University Libraries information literacy learning outcomes*. (Available from the Western

Libraries, Western Washington University, 516 High Street, Bellingham, WA 98225-9103)

Woolf, S.H., Chan, E. C. Y., Harris, R., Sheridan, S. L, Braddock, C. H., Kaplan, R. M., et al. (2005). Promoting informed choice: Transforming health care to dispense knowledge for decision making. *Annals of Internal Medicine. 143*, 293-300.

APPENDIX A

Department of Communication Sciences and Disorders Mission

The Department of Communication Sciences and Disorders is committed to providing a student-centered learning environment of the highest quality where undergraduate and graduate students develop the knowledge, clinical skills, and lifelong learning skills to prepare them for professional careers and advanced study in speech-language pathology and audiology. The faculty and staff are dedicated to engaged excellence as we focus on:

- Fostering the critical thinking, intellectual rigor, curiosity, and creativity that will provide the foundation for ongoing learning about communication and its disorders.
- Providing supervised clinical experiences where students have multiple opportunities to provide high quality client/patient care.
- Creating opportunities for students to understand and engage in research related to normal and disordered communication.
- Promoting an understanding of social, political, and multicultural issues that impact learning, research, and clinical service delivery.
- Encouraging and supporting civic engagement, leadership, and active involvement in campus-life and the broader community.
- Promoting scholarship, educational innovation, and instructional excellence.

APPENDIX B

Summary of Student Feedback Forms for CSD 556: Internet Evaluation and CDS Resources on the Internet

1. I have received library instruction prior to this course:

- None (1)
- As part of a CSD class (11)
- At the Reference Desk (0)
- Other (0)

Questions 2 and 3 were answered on a continuum:

Strongly Disagree   Strongly Agree

1............2............3............4............5

2. The evaluation examples were helpful

- 1 (0)
- 2 (0)
- 3 (1)
- 4 (4)
- 5 (7)

*Comments

- Great stuff, very important for both clinicians and clients.
- More

3. The searching examples were helpful

- 1 (0)
- 2 (0)
- 3 (2)
- 4 (3)
- 5 (7)

Comments)

- The more I can learn about something, the better.
- More

4. I will utilize the content from this instruction session in the future

- 1 (0)
- 2 (0)
- 3 (1)
- 4 (5)
- 5 (6)

Comments

- Heavens yes! Thank you.
- The handout for clients I will definitely use.
- Handouts very helpful.

5. What was the most valuable thing you learned in the library session?

- Using credited sources that will help our clients from becoming frustrated.
- Having handouts and getting info, re: How clients search online was helpful.
- Good, reliable health links to guide patients and our own research.
- Evaluating health Web sites.
- Distinguishing more credible sites.
- Some of the better Web sites to search from (e.g., healthfinder.gov).
- The healthweb pages.
- Awareness; this is something I have never thought about.
- Google vs. Healthfinder, Register.com, and CSD specialized lists!!!! Heard of it, but didn't know how to access...

6. Any comments that you wish to make concerning the class
- Making this class early in the year. (8)
- If it were longer in time instruction and perhaps one quarter sooner (Fall 1st yr grad), but great info, thanks!!
- This would be helpful earlier as well (Perhaps during Voice class in Fall).
- Spread it over 2 sessions. (2)
- Page with good sites.

- This should be done winter quarter, Fall quarter is very difficult. More would be retained during winter quarter.
- As always...Thank you much.

APPENDIX C

A Proposal for a Library Instruction Sequence for Students in the Department of Communication Sciences and Disorders. Submitted to the Communication Sciences and Disorders (CSD) Faculty by Sylvia Tag, Librarian for the Department of CSD.

This proposal suggests the establishment of instruction sessions on library resources and research strategies for the students in the CSD program.

Background

The idea for a sequence of library instruction for CSD students emerged from several different sources. Over the last several years, I have provided library instruction for CSD454 and CSD502. The tremendous value of these sessions is that they are course integrated. The students have assignments and papers that they are working on and they can bring the immediacy of their learning need to the instruction session. This makes for a more meaningful and relevant experience for myself and the students. During the 2002 academic year I wanted to assess the effectiveness of these library research sessions by distributing an end of the quarter evaluation. The 454 library session provides an overview of the scholarly databases for CSD, including how to locate peer-reviewed, scientific research articles. The 502 session reviews some of the 454 content and includes some citation analysis and searching. Comments from the students indicated that the information covered was helpful but they wished that they had received library instruction earlier on in their studies. From my own observations, students varied widely in their research experiences. Some students are regular library users and others are not familiar with the basic protocols for accessing library materials and resources.

Last fall, I had the opportunity to provide sessions for CSD373 and CSD556 courses. The 373 session focused on locating materials in the library, reference materials and using interlibrary loan. This content is mentioned only in passing in 454 and 502, with the exception of interlibrary loan for articles. The 556 session was on medical information on the Internet. Medical information on the Internet is a very timely and important area especially in the area of critical evaluation. Student evaluations echoed themes from other sessions, primarily that a series of sessions early in the program would aid students in their research.

This proposal, based on student feedback, faculty conversations, and my own observations, outlines a library instruction sequence that will help students to acquire and apply research skills and strategies in their CSD coursework at Western and will assist in their preparation for continuing research as practicing clinicians.

Information Literacy Learning Outcomes

The following outcomes are adapted from the Western Libraries Instruction Program
Upper Division Students should be able to:

1. The Social Aspect of Information

- Demonstrate knowledge of the ethics of information use by defining plagiarism and by explaining how and when to give credit for information and ideas from others by appropriately citing sources

2. The Organization of Information

- Describe and distinguish between scholarly and popular publications in the field of communication sciences and disorders
- Describe and distinguish between primary and secondary sources
- Demonstrate an understanding of the difference between controlled/subject vocabulary and free text. For example, MeSH
- Use the library catalog, library online resources and databases to locate reference sources, journal articles and scholarly materials

3. The Research Process

- Construct a logical plan for in-depth research
- Identify and use criteria for evaluating possible sources
- Assess the number and quality of the citations to determine whether the search strategy must be refined
- Demonstrate techniques for writing bibliographic citations for varying formats of materials in correct APA format

Graduate Students should be able to: (everything already mentioned plus)

1. The Social Aspect of Information

- Explain concepts and issues related to censorship, intellectual freedom, and respect for different points of view

2. The Organization of Information

- Use citation indexes and explain how they differ from other indexes

3. The Research Process

- Use the components of Internet sources to choose those most suitable for the information need, using criteria such as currency, reputation of the author, elements of the Web page, etc.
- Explain how people and organizations can be used as information sources
- Recognize that information-seeking is an evolving, non-linear process that involves making a set of choices

Instruction Sessions

- 5 evenings during fall quarter (graduate students)
- 5 evenings during winter quarter (undergraduate students)
- The sessions will be a combination of Lectures and Labs
- There may be short, applied learning assignments between some sessions related to instruction or linked to a course
- Content will include: The library Web site, subject databases, APA citation rules, and Internet resources. In addition the graduate students

Library Resources Beyond the Sessions

- Continuing support by individual or group appointment with the librarian for the department of Communication Sciences & Disorders
- Web pages developed by the library on proper citations formats, CSD reference materials and new acquisitions
- Regularly updated Web page of recommended Internet sources
- Additional course-related instruction as requested

Assessment

- Session evaluations
- End of the quarter evaluations (or evaluations at some future time interval. In other words, finding out if/how students apply the research strategies taught in the library sessions)
- Feedback from CSD Faculty
- Evidence of library instruction in student work (accurate bibliographic citations, critical evaluation of sources, etc.)
- Report prepared by the librarian for the CSD department on the above that is submitted to the CSD faculty.

Appendix

- Student evaluations from CSD 373, 454, 502 and 556
- Complete copy of the Western Library Information Literacy Learning Outcomes
- Web evaluation criteria from The Internet Health Coalition

APPENDIX D

Assignment–Information Seekers and Providers

Purpose

- To reflect on the differing perspectives of information seekers
- To reflect on the differing skills and practices of information seekers
- To reflect on your role as an information provider

Audience

- Your class instructor and colleagues

Process

1. Read the article, *Use of the Internet by parents of pediatric patients.* (Full-text through Library Reserve)

2. Read the article, *Promoting informed choice: Transforming health care to dispense knowledge for decision making.* (Full-text through Library Reserve)
3. Read the article, *Seeking health information on the Internet: Lifestyle choice or bad attack of cyberchondria.* (Full-text through Library Reserve)
4. Write a one-page reflection on how clinicians and patients may differ in terms of perspectives and practices regarding information seeking and retrieval. The Internet provides discussion groups, commercial advertising and research–are there any significant differences between these types of sources? What is your own experience in searching for health information on the Internet?

   a. Typewritten with double-spaced lines of text

   b. If you quote or paraphrase any text from the article you must include a citation.

   c. On a separate page, create a reference list with an APA citation for each article

Assessment

- Thoughtful comments and ideas
- Complete and accurate citations, if applicable, in APA style format
- Reference List in APA style format

Note: All assignments are Pass/Fail. Completion of all assignments is required to pass the course.

APPENDIX E

Assignment–Student Technology Center Publisher Brochure

Purpose

- To become familiar with the services of the Student Technology Center
- To create a publication for distribution to patients and clients

Audience

- The intended target audience for your brochure
- Your instructor and colleagues
- The CSD Department staff and faculty

Process

1. Choose a topic.

2. Create a "brochure" folder on your U:drive

    a. Collect text for your brochure and place it in a "text" sub-folder
    b. Collect images for you brochure and place them in an "images" sub-folder

3. There is a sample brochure on the class Blackboard course site

    a. Some elements you may include in your brochure: borders, images, picture collage, text wrapping, column formatting.
    b. You do not have to include a lot of fancy elements but you must make your brochure interesting and appropriate to the target audience.

4. Be creative!

Assessment

- Completion of the brochure with a focused topic
- Inclusion of several Publisher design elements
- Proper credits: Images, Internet sites, books, articles, etc.
- Your name and date of publication

Note: Turn in TWO copies–I will return one to you and keep one to share with the CSD dept. and future classes. All assignments are pass/fail. Completion of all assignments is required to pass the course.

APPENDIX F

Assignment–Research Strategies: Collecting Resources

Purpose

To demonstrate the ability to locate and retrieve CSD scholarship and research from a variety of sources

Process

1. Select a topic from the *Term Papers–Suggested Topics* handout

2. Follow the guide-sheet–copy and past into a word document

3. Collect resources and include a narrative note as directed for each resource

Criteria for selection of sources

The sources must be from CSD scholarly literature
Date of Publication

- Current–within the last 6 years
- Older sources will be accepted if they are seminal or cited extensively

Research Methodology
- Literature Review of scholarship and/or research
- Meta-analysis of scholarship and/or research
- Clinical Trial
- Controlled Study
- Longitudinal Study
- Quantitative Study
- Empirical Study

Recognized Author or Institution

Assessment

- Completion of the guide-sheet

- Submit the completed guide-sheet via e-mail as an electronic attachment
- Adherence to APA conventions
- Formatting that retains its integrity over e-mail

Note: All assignments are Pass/Fail. Completion of all assignments is required to pass the course.

Guide for Collecting Resources

1. ComDisDome

- Select an article published within the last 6 years
- Article Citation:
- Narrative Notes: What content in the abstract tells you that this is an article you should review? Look at the book and Web–titles anything interesting? Is the article available electronically or in print though the library?
- Narrative:

2. CSA Database of your choice: ERIC–PsychInfo–Medline

- Find an article published in the last 6 years
- Article Citation:
- Narrative Notes: Which database did you choose and why? List the *Descriptor* terms for the article you selected. Refine or broaden your search using *Descriptors*. What was the result? If you choose and article from a journal that is outside the CSD discipline, justify your decision. Is the article available electronically or in print though the library?
- At this point, are you satisfied with the articles you've collected? In other words, if you really had to write a article, would you be changing or modifying your topic at this point? Explain.
- Narrative:

3. Web of Science
- Do a General search for your topic
- Article Citation: Take one of the articles you selected from the ComDisDome or CSA and do a Cited Reference Search. If you can't find the exact article, search the author(s).

- Note the Citation Article (the article that cited your original article):
- Narrative Notes: Were you successful in this database. Explain.
- Narrative:

4. Library Catalog

- Check the library catalog. Keyword Search
- Resource Citation:
- Narrative Notes: List Library of Congress Subject Headings for your topic

5. Your choice: Google Scholar or Google U.S. Government

- Google Scholar–Choose an article or a book that is available online or in print through the library
- Google U.S. Government–Are the laws or legislation that impact your topic?
- Narrative Notes: Which Google index did you choose and why? What is your impression of the results and access to resources?
- Narrative

6. Pubmed, MedlinePlus, or a Web site of your choice

- Do an Internet search for your topic. Make sure you actually search the Web site and reference a particular section or if you link away from primary Web site–cite the Internet source where you finally end up.
- Web site citation:
- Narrative Notes: What kinds of information are available on the Web for your topic? Are clients and patients going to need assistance in understanding the etiology and/or treatment of your topic?

APPENDIX G

Final Essay: Information in the field of Communication Sciences and Disorders

Purpose

In this class, we explore resources that are available for use in your graduate work. The strategies and skills that you acquire through your studies will continue beyond Western when you become practitioners, educators and continuing researchers. Indeed, you are becoming an expert in your field. However, critical thinking is also about being an informed and engaged citizen who understands the political, economic, and cultural issues related to knowledge production, organization and dissemination.

Audience

Course Instructor and the Staff and Faculty of the CSD Dept.

Process

Write a culminating essay that reflects on the following questions:

How is information created, organized, and shared in the field of CSD? Are there any resources that you think are especially important for clinicians and/or clients? Are there elements or aspects of information access that are particularly significant to the discipline and study of CSD? Who are the populations that are affected by the dispersal of information? Clinicians? Researchers? Students? Children? Educators? Parents? Legislators? What are the ethics that shape (or should shape) the sharing of information in educational and medical settings? What are you doing now, as a graduate student, to create habits of knowledge?

Assessment

- 2 pages, double-spaced, paginated
- A bibliography is not required. However, if you quote a source you must provide a citation in APA citation style

The Literature on Academic Integrity and Graduate Students: Issues, Solutions, and the Case for a Librarian Role

Patti Schifter Caravello

INTRODUCTION

Academic dishonesty occurs at all educational levels, including graduate and professional school. Graduate students are expected to comply with their institution's academic integrity rules and the ethical codes of conduct in their chosen disciplines. They face severe consequences if caught cheating or plagiarizing, such as the inability to obtain a research grant, expulsion from the university, or destruction of their chances of entering a profession. Unchecked, dishonest behavior might continue in such careers as law, university teaching, medicine, and business. Faculty, librarians, and university deans assume, to varying degrees, that students enter graduate and professional programs with an understanding of how to use and credit sources appropriately, how and why to avoid plagiarism, misrepresentation, falsification, and fabrication, and the value of adhering to academic honor codes and professional ethics conventions. Further, they assume that training in and understanding of policies and the consequences of transgressions lead to ethical behavior. Empirical research, however, has shown that these assumptions are often false.

Most studies on academic integrity have focused on undergraduates (Ercegovac & Richardson, 2004; McCabe, Treviño, & Butterfield, 2001). While this literature provides the foundation to understand the issues, recent research reveals that graduate students, who are involved in many more types of academic work than undergraduates, face some distinct academic integrity dilemmas and that the concerns vary to some extent by discipline. In an article that challenges the one-size-fits-all approach to information literacy instruction and proposes new roles for librarians as instructors, Simmons (2005) asserts that librarians can be most effective at instruction with undergraduates when they understand the nature of the "disciplinary discourse" characteristic of the field in which the students are working. Swazey, Anderson, and Louis (1993) assert that "understanding the nature of disciplines and departments will help to explain why certain types of ethical problems take place more frequently in some fields and graduate programs than in others" (p. 551). The present survey attempts to bring together the key empirical literature on graduate student academic integrity in order to foster an understanding of the general and discipline-related issues. As information literacy instructors and graduate student consultants, librarians can use this information to develop their teaching and consulting roles as part of the solution.

SCOPE AND METHOD

I searched databases covering a wide range of academic disciplines[1] and reviewed articles primarily from scholarly and academic journals, as well as a selection of books and dissertations to discover: (a) what are the main issues in graduate student academic integrity, (b) what is reported about individual disciplines regarding graduate student academic integrity, and (c) what solutions are suggested that can be instructive to librarians, or include librarians, who teach and consult with graduate students on research and information literacy skills. This survey offers a spectrum of compelling studies, not an exhaustive inventory, published in approximately the last ten years. I have excluded material that more broadly concerns the ethics of professions or the moral development of graduate students where there is no academic integrity connection. To cite a recent trend or event, I have used a few articles from *The Chronicle of Higher Education* although the survey's purpose is to collocate the findings of research studies and articles from scholarly and disciplinary literature rather than news reports. The literature survey is further limited to materials in English, with a concentration on the United States.

RESEARCH THAT PORTRAYS THE ISSUES

Studies of Prevalence and Factors

Although some studies provide data on how many respondents self-report dishonest academic activity, no estimate exists that would categorically answer the question, "What percentage of graduate students cheat?" Figures vary widely depending on the type of study, the type of misconduct, and the disciplines included. The Acadia Institute's Graduate Education Project, a major study conducted in 1990, surveyed two thousand graduate students and as many faculty from 99 departments representing four disciplines (chemistry, civil engineering, microbiology, and sociology). Anderson (1996) reports that over a fifth of the graduate students in this study had witnessed examples of every type of misconduct within their own departments (p. 19), and for some types the percentage was much higher: 63% observed "cheating in coursework" and 31% observed "inappropriately assigning authorship" (p. 18). Based on the Acadia study, Swazey et al. (1993) report that 44%

of graduate students and half the faculty respondents had "been exposed to two or more types" of misconduct (p. 552).

In a dissertation study at a "religiously affiliated university," Wajda-Johnston (2001) found that faculty members greatly underestimate the amount of cheating in which graduate students engage. An article based on this study reports that although 73.1% of graduate student respondents said they had not cheated in graduate school, "when asked if they had engaged in specific dishonest acts, only 24.8% reported that they had not" (Wajda-Johnston, Handal, Brawer, & Fabricatore, 2001, p. 301), that is, about 75% said they had engaged in some academically dishonest behavior. This figure, though based on a small sample, approximates the results of a large scale survey of cheating in which 70% of undergraduates "admit to some cheating" (McCabe, 2005, first bullet). A recent study (McCabe, Butterfield, & Treviño, 2006) found that 47% of non-business graduate students and 56% of business graduate students had cheated in the past year (p. 298). The authors of this article, who have written a great deal about academic integrity, consider this "an alarming rate" (p. 304).

In the Acadia study, Anderson (1996) found that the "general atmosphere" of the academic department has a bigger effect on graduate student misconduct than the department's national rank, apparent faculty commitment to ethics, clear policies, or good mentoring. A climate that respects "traditional norms of research" and fosters a "community of researchers" rather than cutthroat competition has the least misconduct (p. 30), and this holds true for all the departments studied (Anderson, Louis, & Earle, 1999). Although many factors are at play, research on age and academic level of student are pertinent because graduate students are at a higher level and are generally older. In a thoroughgoing analysis of previously conducted research on cheating, Whitley (1998) reports that although ten studies indicate that younger students tend to cheat more than older students, "cheating . . . is essentially uncorrelated with year in college" according to eight other studies that looked at this factor (p. 242). A study of the context of undergraduate cheating (McCabe & Treviño, 1997, not cited in Whitley) also found that older students report less academically dishonest behavior. A few studies (Penzel, 2000; Wajda-Johnston, 2001) say that graduate students cheat less than undergraduates. Respondents in the Wajda-Johnston study were more likely to cheat earlier in their graduate education than later, but another study suggests that students cheat more "the further along [they are in their] academic career" (Kerkvliet & Sigmund, 1999, p. 339). Gender is another factor addressed in some studies of academic dishonesty about which there is no clear consensus. Whitley reviewed many studies that looked at this factor and concluded that in self-report surveys men are more apt to admit to cheating than women and so their rates appear higher, while in observational studies the difference between men and women is much smaller (p. 242). Unlike for undergraduates in several studies that indicate males cheat more, Wajda-Johnston found rates of dishonesty were not related to gender.

Studies reveal that knowledge of policies or even basic ethics training do not succeed in preventing graduate student academic dishonesty (Brown & Kalichman, 1998; Fly, van Bark, Weinman, Kitchener, & Lang, 1997; Penzel, 2000; Tryon, 2000; Wajda-Johnston, 2001). Faculty and students would not always carry out their "ideal response," which is presumably based on knowledge or a sense of the right thing to do, to many hypothetical situations involving reporting acts of cheating by others; their "realistic response" (e.g., not to report) often differs from their ideal (Wajda-Johnston et al., 2001). Teaching assistants in psychology who had more teaching experience were more likely to engage in unethical behavior, including ignoring student cheating, ignoring the "unethical behavior of a faculty member, . . . and [failing] to update lecture material" (Branstetter & Handelsman, 2000, p. 45). Graduate students who teach may find that their "first lesson in graduate school [is] that it is acceptable to cut ethical corners" because so many of them are asked to teach without proper training, experience, or supervision, or to teach subjects they have not mastered, behaviors the graduate students themselves view as unethical (p. 45). This study found that, consistent with earlier studies, graduate students do not always "act in accordance with their beliefs" about and understanding of the ethical issues (p. 48).

Rationales for Academic Dishonesty

Major reasons given by graduate students who commit unethical academic behaviors are: academic pressures/workload/intense stress (Anderson, 2002; Love & Simmons, 1998; Sheard & Dick, 2003; Wajda-Johnston, 2001), a competitive edge/the need for better grades in order to get better jobs or move into better graduate schools (Brown, 1995; Brown & Kalichman, 1998; Wajda-Johnston, 2001), pressure or coercion by powerful faculty members (Reybold, 2002), student observations that faculty cut corners (Brown & Kalichman, 1998; Lerman, 2001), lack of training (Branstetter & Handelsman, 2000; Hsu, 2003; Love & Simmons, 1998; Reybold, 2002), the perception that their peers cheat (McCabe, Butterfield, & Treviño, 2006), and the slim chance of getting caught (Brown, 1995; McCabe, Butterfield, & Treviño, 2006). But motivations can vary by discipline: Penzel (2000) notes that grades remain important to law students during graduate school because of the kind of competition they will face in the job market, whereas grades are not as important for psychology graduate students. Penzel found low rates of cheating (based on self-report) among law and psychology graduate students, whose values related to learning influence them to behave ethically. In a study of the socialization of future professors, Reybold (2002) reports that because prolific publication is valued at universities, ethics is sometimes a casualty in a pressurized culture that seems ambivalent to ethics. Some students relate that faculty or situations encourage them to act unethically in an atmosphere where "ethical dilemmas may become stumbling blocks to promotion and tenure" (p. 43). Some students fear losing a research assistantship or the good graces of particular faculty members, or they fear retaliation "if they resist their . . . advisor's management of their research" (p. 46). Underscoring difficult power relationships and the vulnerability some graduate students feel, Wiener (2005) describes a particularly egregious case in which a faculty member had a long history of pressuring mainly female graduate students to do personal favors or else lose their funding or not have their dissertations signed.

Plagiarism

Estimates are not available on the prevalence of plagiarism among graduate students as a whole, but some data emerge. In a study that used the Google search engine to detect plagiarism in 210 master's theses (McCullough & Holmberg, 2005), "potential occurrences of plagiarism were found in 57 of 210 (27.14%) theses" (p. 438). Online sources from which the graduate students had plagiarized included articles, abstracts, various kinds of Web sites, personal homepages, encyclopedias, and government pages. In 60% of the suspect theses, Google identified more than one "long phrase" match, possibly indicating a pattern of behavior rather than an isolated incidence. In the Acadia study, "nearly a third of faculty [respondents] claim to have observed [graduate] student plagiarism" in the four disciplines studied, the percentage being higher in engineering and sociology (Swazey et al., 1993, p. 545). Sheard and Dick (2003) report that over one-third of their information technology graduate student survey respondents had committed acts of what they call "minor plagiarism (copying from a book or Web site, resubmission)" (p. 49).

Baggaley and Spencer (2005) delve into the motivations, actions, and defenses offered in the case of a single graduate student "serial plagiarist" in a distance education setting. In the end (and after expulsion from the program) the student confessed his design for graduate work, which was to employ regularly and without attribution the passages and quotations from a homemade database compiled from various online sources. But this admission came only after a long period of accusation, indignation, misplaced blame, and claims of confusion and ignorance. In analyzing two graduate students' research processes and participation in a seminar, Prior (1998b) found that the one who proceeded with the research in a structural, not deeply engaged way ended up plagiarizing and doing a poor job of citation in her thesis, while the student who had more intensely and seriously engaged in her research and seminar on many levels used and synthesized other authors' texts more properly in her thesis and cited more sources. In one section of a book on the various components of academic misconduct, Decoo (2002) analyzes in depth the specific forms of plagiarism he found in a doctoral dissertation completed at a European university where, even with Decoo's protestations of plagiarism and lack of quality or original research in the thesis, the doctoral degree was still conferred, and with honors. The chapter (pp. 61-116) shines a bright light on deceptive and careless writing and could serve as an illustrative lesson to graduate students on unethical practices in writing a thesis.

In a postmodern reassessment of plagiarism, some authors have suggested that because plagiarism is a word fraught with moral judgment and its definition not always clear, the word should be reserved for the most outright misrepresentations (such as putting one's name on a article written by someone else), and textual practices should be examined more analytically. Students' insufficient knowledge of the subject they are writing about and a lack of guidance about the use of sources result in over-reliance on source text. The desire to be part of the academic "discourse community," not a tendency to cheat, leads to "patchwriting" (Howard, 1999, p. 7), i.e., the verbatim or slightly altered use of text from one or more sources pieced together often without citation (p. xvii). Rather than see plagiarism as a moral transgression, these theorists view it as a "contested concept" (Angélil-Carter, 2000, p. 2) and patchwriting a means of "learning through . . . mimicry" (Howard, 1999, p. xviii). They challenge the notion of originality (Angélil-Carter, 2000, pp. 18-20), and focus on the difficult process of "developing authorial voice" (p. 104). Chandrasoma, Thompson, and Pennycook (2004) would "do away with the notion of

plagiarism in favour of an understanding of transgressive and nontransgressive intertextuality"
(p. 171). Reframing the problem leads to a focus on teaching rather than punishment (Howard, 2001) and a deeper understanding of the student perspective. Most of these authors focus on undergraduate writing. Abasi, Akbari, and Graves (2006), however, studied the writing processes and products of five Canadian ESL graduate students and concluded by explicitly supporting the reframed conceptual approach and declaring that plagiarism is "essentially the result of students' failure to represent themselves as writers who should make a novel contribution . . . through critically engaging with sources" (p. 114). Although these are not conventional takes on the problem of plagiarism, they challenge instructors to concentrate on student writing processes and to teach about the use of sources in the context of a discipline, actions that many would agree are needed.

International Graduate Students and Plagiarism

With many international students at U.S. universities, the issue arises of their learning new norms and conventions for the use of others' words and ideas in their writing. Rinnert and Kobayashi (2005) explore Japanese students' attitudes and understanding of paraphrasing, quoting, and attribution when writing in their first language and how this affects how they handle such practices in their second language (English). The part of this study that included Japanese graduate students indicates that the only way in which they differ from undergraduates is that they are more likely to see proper citation as important. About half of the graduate students gave "survival strategies" as a reason for plagiarism and–perhaps more surprising–15% gave "have the same idea, or understand/agree with the writer" as a reason. Although 75% said that "plagiarism was never unavoidable" (p. 42), how they defined plagiarism differs from U.S. conventions, and they expressed a lack of training in this area. According to another study, in which Chinese graduate students in the sciences and social sciences were interviewed, plagiarism is seen as more acceptable for an article in a popular magazine or newspaper or for class assignments than for publication in a scholarly journal (Bloch, 2001). Barks (2001) states that "the development of appropriate [textual] borrowing practices presents a daunting challenge for many ESL writers" (p. 246). Barks explores the connection of reading to writing in a second language and how this varies in the "discourse communities" of different disciplines. She describes methods for teaching ESL graduate students the textual borrowing practices for their disciplines that are acceptable in the U.S. The study by Hsu (2003) affirms that rigorous training in citation and paraphrasing makes a significant difference in preventing plagiarism by ESL graduate students, while simple knowledge of the rules does not have this effect.

Authorship Issues

The relationship between graduate student and professor or thesis advisor can lead to questions about who should be given author credit in the final product, and instances when faculty use graduate student text without attribution. *The Chronicle of Higher Education* reports news of such problems (e.g., Bartlett & Smallwood, 2004). Tryon, Bishop, and Hatfield (2002) surveyed doctoral students in school psychology to discover their opinions about scenarios in which the idea for a dissertation topic was suggested by the faculty advisor, how desirable this is, and whether authorship credit for a subsequent article should ethically belong to the student alone, or both the student and the faculty advisor, and if the latter, in which order. The study found that these graduate students believe it is "more ethical [for them] to develop their own dissertation ideas," (p. 6) but that even if the idea originated with the faculty advisor, it is more ethical for the doctoral student to be the sole author of the dissertation and the sole or first author of any article resulting from the dissertation, "even when the advisor . . . wrote the article," which is technically in keeping with the ethical principles of the American Psychological Association (p. 6). Rose and Fischer (1998) found that graduate students in the sciences and social sciences, responding to various vignettes in which the professor always ends up as the first author, showed reluctance to report authorship problems to authorities. The existence of an authorship policy affected women's ethical ratings in only one of the vignettes, and did not affect men's responses at all, which is notable since honor codes and clear policies are sometimes seen as part of the remedy for academic integrity problems.

Fishman (1999) describes a highly contentious case of a Cornell nutrition and psychology professor using the award-winning research of his thesis advisee to get a grant, continue, and take credit for the research. The student accused the professor of stealing her ideas and forcing her out of her research project, while the professor denied this, said the work was collaborative, and claimed he was being defamed. While Cornell ultimately–but not unequivocally–sided with the professor, this complex "case illustrates both the ambiguities of intellectual-property ownership and the vulnerability of graduate students" (p. 44). In addressing the mentorship role of faculty toward their graduate students, Kennedy (1997) notes that similar practices are, to varying degrees, "perfectly routine" in academia but are surprising to uninitiated graduate students, who see these practices as wrong (p. 99). Kennedy provides examples of how conventions differ from discipline to discipline in such details as whose name appears first, whether the professor's name always appears regardless of contribution, and even the meaning of co-authorship. Lerman (2001) describes the definitions of authorship developed in the disciplines of law, medicine, psychology, and by the American Association of University Professors, and the significant differences between them due to the kind of research and writing done in various disciplines.

RESEARCH THAT ILLUSTRATES DISCIPLINARY DISTINCTIONS

Empirical studies of graduate students in a single discipline appear for only some fields. Notably absent are studies focusing on academic integrity of graduate students in the disciplines of the humanities where writing is so central to the academic enterprise. This is all the more surprising against the backdrop of mass media exposés of plagiarists and falsifiers who are professional historians, writers, and journalists. Some books and articles indicate the passions in academia surrounding issues of honesty in the humanities and writing professions, even if they do not focus on or provide data about graduate students. Rather than omit these fields, it seems pertinent to mention a few articles that can aid an understanding of disciplinary issues. For example, Robin (2004) describes and analyzes recent academic scandals in the fields of history and anthropology. In Rebecca Moore Howard's sometimes controversial articles on plagiarism, she tackles the issue in the context of teaching English to undergraduates (e.g., Howard, 1999). A short piece by Gorney (2001) is "an open letter" on integrity to graduate students of journalism, written in response to a falsified story published in a local newspaper by a newly minted journalist. Journalism is also the context of Lampert's (2004) plagiarism program with undergraduates. In a special section of an issue of *The Journal of American History*, six short articles discuss the ethics of historians. One of these (Lapsansky, 2004) proposes that new history graduate students undergo a ceremony "akin to the ritual 'white coating' that happens when students enter medical school" (para. 15) in order to more persuasively implant in future historians an ethical commitment. The sections below are for disciplines in which empirical studies have been done.

Psychology

Because graduate students in psychology have direct contact with clients, ethical issues revolve mainly around competence, proper procedures, confidentiality, and client-therapist boundaries, but academic integrity issues also arise. Vacha-Haase (1995) found that 11% percent of the graduate psychology programs in her study had terminated students for academic dishonesty (p. 111) which continued to be an ongoing problem for over a quarter of those programs (p. 123), and that overall, 12% of the programs were experiencing problems with graduate student academic dishonesty (p. 121). In a survey of school psychology graduate program directors, the most frequent violations reported were related to "confidentiality, competence, and professional and academic honesty" (Tryon, 2000, p. 277). The issue that the directors thought would be most problematic for students was "reporting ethical violations by other graduate students" (p. 276). Interestingly, directors said students do not find the other issues problematic, including "taking publication credit only for work performed," "resisting pressures to cheat on exams," and "when writing papers, giving appropriate citations"(p. 276)–even though the administrators reported incidents involving these issues. In an earlier, exploratory survey of directors of graduate psychology programs, respondents viewed the most serious incidents as those that could directly affect clients; these signaled "a failure to understand. . . the core ethical values of the profession" (Fly et al., 1997, p. 494). But other kinds of violations that showed dishonesty, including "plagiarism or falsification of data" (15% of the total violations reported), misrepresenting credentials, and integrity breaches, indicated that some students "did not understand the importance of honesty and integrity in maintaining trusting human relationships, a central value in psychology training" (p. 494).

In an investigation of collaborations between psychology faculty and students that resulted in articles being published, Sandler and Russell (2005) found that "a third of all [604] respondents felt they have or may have been involved in a perceived [authorship] incident" (p. 77) either as faculty members or in the past as students collaborating with faculty. Further, despite the few incidents annually reported to the American Psychological Association, the study found that authorship problems occur at a "high rate" and that respondents had hardly reported any (only 3.7%) of the incidents to authorities. Oberlander and Barnett (2005) describe ethical problems and guidelines for psychology graduate students who teach and develop multiple roles and relationships with their students that can lead to academic integrity problems, among others.

Social Work

Similar to the literature in psychology, articles on the ethics and ethical training of social work graduate students focus on professional practice. Collins and Amodeo (2005), however, report on a project at one graduate school of social work that addressed the problem of plagiarism. The article describes a process for defining, helping faculty to respond to, and helping students understand the meaning and consequences of plagiarism. It includes a logical approach to the levels and types of plagiarism and of the "mediating factors" such as "severe stress" and "acceptance of responsibility" (p. 535) that can affect the response to a case of plagiarism. The faculty committee involved in this project considered the "relative importance of practice performance versus academic performance" (p. 537) in social work, a profession that is mainly situated in the field and clinic, and they held that plagiarism nonetheless called into doubt a graduate "student's ability to become an ethical social worker" (p. 537).

Education

In a qualitative study on what contributes to unethical academic behaviors of first-year education graduate students, Love and Simmons (1998) found that all six of the students interviewed were aware of cheating by their classmates or had cheated or plagiarized themselves, and that the main contributing factor to cheating was the pressures brought on by grades, time, and workload. The other "external" factor was the perception that professors tend to ignore acts of cheating rather than go to the trouble of reporting them, and the students saw this as a kind of "permission" to cheat. There was a shifting of blame to the professors, e.g., if students worked collaboratively on a project that was supposed to be done independently, a dishonest practice, the attitude was that the professor ought to have required that the work be done in class where there is more supervision. Interestingly, these respondents had chosen the profession of teaching or counseling and might one day be in the teaching role in a similar situation. "Negative personal attitudes," the lack of intention to cheat or plagiarize, and a low ability to do graduate work were the "internal" factors seen as contributing to cheating. This study suggests interesting factors and rationales, but it is limited in that it looked at very few students early in their graduate years. Education doctoral student respondents in the Reybold (2002) study reported that they had little ethics training or knowledge of policies specific to conducting research in education, and that participating as a researcher taught them the most about these issues. They reported problems with negotiating authorship, intimidation by powerful faculty, and dissertation committee composition. In another study, education graduate students watched a video about research that had been proven to contain falsified data, and then answered a questionnaire. Results showed that "males were significantly more likely to be surprised by cheating . . . than females" (Newman and Waechter, 2000, p. 5) and they also saw a greater need than the women in the study to improve their ability to avoid unethical practices in research.

Sociology

Significant disciplinary differences were noted in some areas in the Acadia study, in which sociology was the only non-science discipline, and the distinctions identified are therefore only by comparison with the sciences. Graduate students in sociology reported the lowest amount of faculty mentoring of the four disciplines, the lowest "level of community" and among the highest "levels of conflict and competition" (Anderson, 1996, p. 25) in their departments. More than science faculty, sociology faculty tend to support normative research practices rather than "counternorms" (p. 24), and 69% felt strongly that they have "collective responsibility" for graduate student conduct (p. 25), though this percentage was lower than for two of the three science fields. Over 40% of the sociology faculty had "detected plagiarism among their graduate students" (Swazey et al. 1993, p. 545), although they "report[ed] significantly less" data falsification by graduate students than did faculty in the sciences (p. 545). The sociology students and faculty in this study reported more exposures than informants in the other disciplines to "interpersonal misconduct" (as distinct from research or employment misconduct), including sexual harassment, discrimination, and power issues. As sociologists study similar phenomena in society, this finding seems surprising but could be a result of heightened sensitivity among this group to such issues. Anderson et al. (1999) found, however, that this particular disciplinary difference disappeared statistically when the authors "control[led] for department characteristics" (p. 226).

Prior (1998a) analyzes the output of a group of sociology graduate students in a seminar in which they worked collaboratively on a research project. Even with authorship rules established at the start, negotiations ensued, and conflicts arose related to writing and author credit. Prior found it "difficult to untangle whose ideas and whose work a particular text represented" (p. 161) when he looked at the drafts, the principle investigator's substantive changes to them, and the final texts. Furthermore, some students received author credit even though they contributed no writing, and others received no credit although they had collected and coded data for the project. Prior suggests that authorship credit "seemed to reflect disciplinary and sociocultural (e.g., gendered) constructions of work" (p. 165); two of the three graduate students not given author credit were responsible for the less visible data tasks and were women. By focusing on the inner workings of a research team, Prior sheds light on various problems of collaborative research and writing that apparently arise in many disciplines.

Business

A survey by Brown (1995) indicated that graduate business students are about as ethical as undergraduate business students surveyed in previous studies, even though the graduate students saw themselves as more ethical. Eighty percent of respondents participated "in at least one unethical practice more than infrequently" (Conclusion para. 1). There were five behaviors that over 20% of the students said they did "more than infrequently" including getting and sharing information about exams, working collaboratively on individual projects, and "padding a bibliography" (Results para. 5). Respondents engaged less in behaviors they viewed as most unethical, such as misrepresenting someone else's work as their own or copying during exams. In a later study of business students, in which about one quarter of the respondents were graduate students, Nonis and Swift (2001) found "a high correlation between the frequency of cheating at college and the frequency of cheating at work" (p. 75) for both graduate and undergraduate business students. The relationship between college and workplace dishonesty held even when results were controlled for age and gender (given that younger and male respondents were more academically dishonest and "tolerant of workplace dishonesty" than female and older students, p. 74). Possibly owing to their longer work experience, the graduate student respondents judged a third of the unethical work behaviors in the survey as more dishonest than did the undergraduates. McCabe, Butterfield, and Treviño (2006) report that cheating is more prevalent among MBA students than non-business graduate student respondents. For these highly competitive business students, steeped in a "bottom-line mentality" (p. 295), the most important factor is the perception that other business students cheat. Neither the possibility of severe penalties nor a good grasp of university policies about academic integrity were important influences on them. The authors offer many suggestions to remedy the situation that require action by the faculty and integration into the curriculum, including guidelines about collaborative work and a "modified honor code" that would stress professional business conduct rather than punishment (p. 303).

Martin (2005) found that the use of detection software Turnitin.com was an effective deterrent in reducing plagiarism by graduate business students who were aware that the software would be used and that it had discovered plagiarism in prior semesters. In the first of the project's five semesters, plagiarism had been detected in 21 out of 39 papers to varying extents ("from 5% to over 50% of the words," p. 151), but incidents of plagiarism were significantly lower in the last three semesters. One of the reasons the graduate business students in the Brown (1995) study gave for cheating was the unlikelihood of getting caught; the Martin study achieved a significant effect by increasing detection and thereby removing this reason.

Law

Issues that arise in the field of law over attribution of sources and authorship credit center on the contradictions between what is acceptable in academic legal writing and what is acceptable in the practice of law. Problems also stem from the fact that many law schools lack clear definitions of, effective training about, and consistent sanctions for plagiarism. LeClercq (1999b) and Lerman (2001) both describe conventions for law school, law review, and other scholarly writing as similar to the standards for academic writing in other fields in which using other writers' words without attribution is considered plagiarism. Lerman, however, views as a "double standard" (p. 488) the fact that law faculty often use the writing of their law student research assistants without attribution and are not punished for this, while a law student could be dismissed from law school for a similar act. In the academic environment, Lerman sees professors' use of law student writing in their own published work as a dishonest practice and a possible "abuse of power" (p. 471). Practicing lawyers, on the other hand, routinely use standard forms, law clerks' writing, other lawyers' briefs, and judges' opinions in their own briefs and filings without attribution, and this practice is acceptable because, unlike for scholarly writing, authorship and originality are not important in court documents (LeClercq, 1999a). Yarbrough (1996) decries the "mixed messages" law professors send students regarding their lack of acknowledgement of student contributions to their writing and the difference between academic writing and writing in the practice of law.

Based on a 1996 study, LeClercq (1999b) reports that law schools, particularly higher ranked ones, offer students very little training on these issues because they assume that new students already know the rules. This is a dangerous assumption and "the problem of plagiarism in American law schools is reaching a crisis point" (p. 237). Denial of the problem and failure to address it systematically have led to inconsistent definitions and sanctions in law schools, reluctance to report transgressions, and reversals of judgments against students based on due process–which is ironic in a field comprised of experts on the legal system who therefore "should have the clearest and most coherent policies" but "they don't" (LeClercq, 1999a, p. 196). Gerdy (2004) describes faculty views of software for detecting law student plagiarism, including the benefits and some disadvantages, such as "alienating students," the appearance of a "quick fix" to a big problem, and the incompleteness of the sources checked by the software (pp. 439-440). Both Gerhardt (2006) and the Legal Writing Institute (2003) offer lessons and examples for law students on how to avoid plagiarism and what constitutes good paraphrasing and citation in academic writing.

Sciences and Engineering

Academic integrity in the sciences is tied to honesty in the conduct of scientific research; the problems of doing science right and the truthful production of lab results are intertwined in the literature with the honest reporting of those results whether for course work, publication, or financial gain. An article about why undergraduates falsify data posits that even graduate students sometimes "cook" data in an effort to make the results match what they think beforehand is the correct solution (Lawson, Lewis, & Birk, 1999). In one study, first-year doctoral students' ideas of what is normative in science related mainly to specific tasks rather than to an understanding of the context of their disciplines or of higher education "beyond their own departments" (Anderson, 2002, p. 24). Parrish (2004) studied the cases of graduate student academic misconduct that had come before the Office of Research Integrity and the National Science Foundation (NSF) between 1989 and 1999. Most cases involved falsification of data, fabrication of results, and plagiarism, and many cases were the result of "sting" operations to catch students in the act of falsifying–a "unique" investigative method in the sciences not typically used in other fields (p. 487)–but very few cases ended in a finding of misconduct. Those who were found to have transgressed faced sanctions from the federal government, such as a halt to funding, in addition to sanctions from their universities, e.g., degrees withheld or revoked. Langlais (2006) reports on a study done by the American Physical Society in which 39% of respondents who had recently obtained their doctorates had "as graduate students or postdoctoral fellows . . . observed or had personal knowledge of ethical violations" (para. 4).

Since 1990 the National Institutes of Health (NIH) has mandated research integrity training for graduate students on training grants as a prerequisite to NIH funding. Still, Brown and Kalichman (1998) found that this has not increased ethics training (p. 491). They report that having had formal courses or informal discussions with the thesis advisor did not predict the students would behave more ethically. Some studies (Mathur, 2002; Swazey et al., 1993) indicate that informal methods are seen as most important to conveying academic norms in a discipline, yet Brown and Kalichman (1998) and Bird (1999) report that science graduate students actually spend very little time with faculty discussing ethics. Mathur found that graduate students want their departments to help them with ethical issues but that this help is not forthcoming, and they typically ask other students when a question arises. Schrag, Ferrell, Weil, and Fiedler (2003) provide an interesting case study and commentaries to use in training science graduate students about research integrity; the complete set of scenarios developed as part of a larger, NSF-funded project is available online (Online Ethics Center, 2005). Rytting and Schowen (1998) provide an outline and other details for a scientific integrity course for chemistry graduate students. Brainard (2006) describes recent efforts by the Council of Graduate Schools to develop new approaches and "best practices" for training graduate students in scientific ethics, even as they grapple with the effectiveness of such training.

In the McCullough and Holmberg (2005) study, the highest incidence of plagiarism, ranging from about 38-44%, occurred in the various subdisciplines of engineering (p. 438). Earlier, Swazey et al. (1993) had a similar finding (p. 545). In the last two years, articles in *The Chronicle of Higher Education* have recorded an explosive series of events at Ohio University's Russ College of Engineering and Technology. A mechanical-engineering graduate student in 2004 discovered plagiarism in a number of completed theses. After many attempts by the student to expose the problems, eventually an investigative committee found a pattern of plagiarism in the mechanical engineering department going back twenty years and recommended that the head of the department be fired (Wasley, 2006). Perhaps engineering graduate students are more at home with numbers than with writing, or they are highly competitive like the business students who also show a high rate of academic dishonesty, but the literature does not explain why some studies show a higher incidence of plagiarism among this group.

Medicine

In the field of medicine, as in psychology and social work, ethical issues involving patients are seen as more serious than those involving academic dishonesty. Baldwin, Daugherty, Rowley, and Schwarz (1996) surveyed second-year students and found a far lower rate of self-reported cheating (4.7%) than previous studies had found, although 39% of respondents reported that they had witnessed others cheating. Men were more willing than women to cheat if certain they would not be caught and were more likely to say that cheating is due to the competitive atmosphere, although there was no gender difference in self-reported medical school cheating. Since 82% of those who reported that they had cheated also admitted to cheating in lower levels of schooling, this was seen as the "best single predictor" for medical school cheating (p. 270), but the authors emphasize that most prior cheaters do not cheat in medical school. These results and student attitudes were similar to a study in which 5.5% of optometry students admitted to cheating in optometry school and about two thirds of the admitted cheaters had cheated during their previous education (Werner, Heiberger, Feldman, & Johnston, 2000). About a fifth of those who applied for a residency program in pediatrics in one study misrepresented their credentials by listing on their applications articles they had supposedly written but whose existence could not be verified (Bilge, Shugerman, & Robertson, 1998). This study also found that all the applicants to a pediatrics fellowship program who "claimed authorship of publications had made at least one misrepresentation" (p. 532). The authors did not inquire whether the applicants had engaged in other academic dishonesty while in medical school, but it would not be surprising, given the connections made in the other articles between prior and later cheating.

The respondents in the Baldwin et al. (1996) study were unclear about what the appropriate response to cheating should be. Osborn (2000) describes an incident in which a first-year medical student submitted a article written by someone else, and discusses the strong disagreements over the resulting punishments. As the course was seen as unimportant, no patient care was involved, and the article was not for publication, some students felt that lower standards should apply, while other students and faculty saw this as a clear case of cheating and grounds for dismissal. Ethical issues in patient care frequently appear in studies of academic integrity. A study of medical students at Johns Hopkins (Dans, 1996) found that fourth-year respondents felt more strongly than first-year students that medical school cheating makes physicians less trustworthy, though many felt this about only certain types of cheating, such as falsifying lab data, other patient related practices, and cheating that resulted in personal gain (p. S71). This study found that 23% of fourth-year medical students admitted to cheating. Articles that present ethical issues in dental school from the perspective of administrators, faculty, and/or students (Koerber et al., 2005; Tankersley, 1997) help to clarify the various views of the different players, including opinions about the value of ethics training. In a quest to define equitable punishment, Teplitsky (2002) studied how Canadian dental faculty and students view penalties for academic dishonesty, and found that students demonstrate more liberal views than faculty. The role of honor codes in dental (Turner & Beemsterboer, 2003) and medical (Gabbay, 1999) education is seen as influential to instill ethical values in students and to clarify sanctions.

SOLUTIONS FOR GRADUATE STUDENT ACADEMIC DISHONESTY

Solutions Suggested in the Literature

Most if not all articles cited above call for more, or more effective, ethics or research integrity training. As noted earlier, several studies indicate that having taken an ethics course is not a decisive factor in graduate student misconduct. The call for more such courses therefore may not be based on the research but rather on a strong feeling that the remedy must somehow lie in education or that training can be improved. Graduate programs usually do not offer ethics courses (Anderson, Louis, & Earle, 1999; Reybold, 2002) and students are left to learn about ethics in informal ways, on their own, or "via a mentor or apprenticeship model, which has proven to be inadequate" (Branstetter & Handelsman, 2000, p. 30). Over two-thirds of psychology graduate student instructors in the Branstetter & Handelsman study thought that they should have to take a course in ethics before being allowed to teach, and almost half believed a special ethics code for teaching assistants was warranted. Whitley and Keith-Spiegel (2001) also advocate training on academic integrity for graduate students who teach. It is certain that ethics cannot be taught in a single lesson or course, but must be infused in the training over time using multiple methods, and through experience, in order to overcome prior attitudes about cheating (Nonis & Swift, 2001).

Handbooks on how to succeed in graduate school, conduct research, and earn an advanced degree typically include sections on academic integrity, intellectual property, and issues that arise for graduate student teaching assistants (e.g., Brinkley et al., 1999; Elphinstone & Schweitzer, 1998; and Vesilind, 2000). In an analysis of the coverage of ethics in criminal justice textbooks used by graduate and undergraduate students, McSkimming, Sever, and King (2000) conclude that while some topics are fairly well-represented, particularly protection of human subjects, others are given short shrift, such as "plagiarism, forging of data, Institutional Review Boards, authorship rank, and . . . journal editing and grant-writing" (p. 58), areas which are especially important to graduate students. They recommend that new textbooks do a more thorough job with these topics.

Besides more and better training, suggestions for addressing graduate student academic dishonesty include development and dissemination of explicit university policies on plagiarism and other academic integrity issues. LeClercq (1999b) describes an ideal policy as one that would include plagiarism definitions, examples of acceptable paraphrasing, rules about collaborative work, the perils of using e-resources, and clear information on sanctions. Baldwin et al. (1996) suggest that clear standards could help students know what to do when they observe others cheating. Another solution suggested is the development of a climate in the academic department in which honesty, community, and research norms are valued and competition and conflict are minimized (Dans, 1996; Anderson, 1996; Anderson et al., 1999). McCabe, Butterfield, and Treviño suggest establishing a "culture of integrity and responsibility" in which the benefits of ethical behavior are emphasized in an ongoing, "community-building" process (p. 302). Faculty members should act as role models for graduate students with whom they work closely (Cabral-Cardoso, 2004; Nonis & Swift, 2001) and exhibit "high standards of ethical behavior" (Nonis & Swift, 2001, p. 76). Likewise, faculty should consistently abide by university policies to report instances of dishonesty so students are certain that there will be consequences (p. 75) and to convince or reassure students that it is right to report breaches (McCabe, Butterfield, & Treviño, 2006). A clear and fair "plagiarism grading plan" (Martin, 2005, p. 152), in which the amount of plagiarism found by detection software directly affects the grade, is another suggestion. LeClercq (1999b) also advocates a grading policy related to plagiarism found in law students' papers. Some suggest using Turnitin.com (Baggaley & Spencer, 2005; Martin, 2005) and other detection software or Google (McCullough & Holmberg, 2005).

The Case for a Librarian Role

Librarian roles in information literacy continue to evolve, and librarians who serve, teach, and consult with graduate students can develop a substantive role in helping them become knowledgeable about academic integrity as part of information literacy, which, according to the Association of College and Research Libraries (2000), includes the ethics of using and citing information, not only finding and evaluating it. In recent library literature, several articles suggest an instructional role for librarians with undergraduates in the area of plagiarism (Auer & Krupar, 2001; Boden & Carroll, 2006; Hamilton, 2003; Jackson, 2006; Lampert, 2004; Wood, 2004). Earlier, Altman (1997) and Walters (1997) addressed the problem facing users when plagiarized or fabricated publications become part of the library's collections and what the librarian's responsibilities related to this might be, including user instruction and collection monitoring. Despite the fact that "bibliographic instruction" incorporated the concept of critical thinking since at least the early 1980s, Walters cites interviews conducted with librarians in 1995 indicating that many did not think it was their place to address critical thinking with students about what they read or to advocate vigilance because false or unreliable materials might be in the library (p. 103). The fact that most librarians now routinely incorporate this into information literacy instruction is evidence of their changing role in areas once considered solely the purview of the teaching faculty.

Not surprisingly, because librarians have not yet taken on this role in large numbers, none of the disciplinary literature on graduate students mentions librarians as partners in the effort to reduce or deter plagiarism and other ethical breaches. An article by a Rutgers English instructor (Hall, 2005), however, emphasizes a community approach to educating undergraduates about plagiarism, and suggests that librarians play a role in helping to "develop and disseminate materials for instructors to use in an anti-plagiarism learning module" (Principle I, activity 1). He advocates that university staff who interact with students individually, including librarians, take special training to better understand how students perceive plagiarism and how best to weave instruction into interactions with them. Most notably, Hall proposes that faculty should

> involve the library staff in training students not just to find sources, but to evaluate them for appropriateness for a given project, and to use them effectively and honestly in their own arguments. Information literacy must be a core goal of all contemporary universities, and anti-plagiarism efforts need to be a key component of any such initiative. (Hall, 2005, Principle III, activity 11)

Like the articles in the library literature cited above, Hall places the librarian role in educating undergraduates about plagiarism squarely in the context of information literacy. The context for a librarian role with graduate students would be no different, even if some of the approaches to teaching would vary in order to focus on the perspective of the discipline and the more advanced student.

Bird (1998) says that "practicing researchers" are the most important guides graduate students have regarding research ethics because they know the "ethical values of their discipline," and they therefore "provide credibility" (p. 177). The burden for training may rest primarily with the faculty, but it does not need to rest solely with them. On their own and in partnership with faculty, librarians can bring expertise and other benefits to academic integrity training of graduate students. First, many academic librarians are subject experts, have advanced subject degrees, or over time have developed in-depth knowledge about their assigned subject areas and literatures. With this knowledge, they advise graduate students about research in their disciplines, keep up with new scholarship, and develop specialized library collections–and in these ways remain close to and aware of the way research is conducted and reported in the discipline. Second, many academic librarians write for publication and have conducted library, survey, and/or disciplinary research, making them "practicing researchers" who can bring first-hand experience to the discussion or the training. Third, in addition to their discipline-related knowledge, many librarians keep abreast of emerging issues in scholarly publishing, intellectual property, plagiarism, and citation styles, making librarians as aware as faculty of matters that directly affect the format and ethical dissemination of scholarly work. The final major point in the case for a librarian role in addressing academic integrity is that librarians are able to engage students on these sensitive issues in a non-threatening context. Librarians do not usually assign grades, and they have no power in terms of a student's graduate work or thesis. Librarians who advise and teach graduate students in individual consultations, over e-mail, in online tutorials, Web sites, or the classroom are perhaps in a better position than faculty or deans to convey the information as colleagues or partners rather than as university authorities. This can prompt a more open, uninhibited dialogue in which students can more freely air their concerns and reveal their lack of knowledge.

In the same way that library and online collections have to respond to graduate student needs in a research library, library instructional services need to be customized for graduate students. Because of the kind of academic work these students do, it is logical and appropriate for instruction to incorporate academic integrity topics. Caravello (2006) describes a workshop on avoiding plagiarism for graduate students at UCLA, developed with the dean of students, that has been given as part of the new graduate student orientation, as a course-related session, and as a free-standing offering at the library. Bird's (1998) discussion of the advantages and disadvantages of various training formats can also assist librarians considering approaches to instruction in this area. Taking advantage of the general lack of training and the expressed need for it, the necessity and benefits of partnering with others interested in academic integrity, and the various remedies proposed in the literature, librarians can experiment and contribute by:

- Actively collaborating with faculty and deans to initiate, situate, and develop better training that is coordinated with the students' research experiences and graduate curriculum. This could include multiple opportunities for training and discussion in settings such as graduate student orientations, presentations in graduate courses, online modules, and workshops and individual consultation services in the library, academic departments, and writing center.
- Experimenting with techniques to incorporate academic integrity content tailored to the discipline into information literacy instruction and course assignments. This would require knowledge of the disciplinary issues, and should use active learning techniques and opportunities for follow-up to instruction. Integrating an academic

integrity learning experience into course assignments necessitates collaboration with the faculty instructor.

- Sponsoring faculty and graduate student forums and symposiums to encourage open discussion of plagiarism and other academic integrity issues (Hall, 2005). This could heighten awareness, increase understanding of the issues, and lead to dialogue and learning. It could also result in the library's becoming a partner or even a place for this discussion and librarians being recognized as allies in developing solutions.
- Developing informative or didactic, self-help, online aids at the graduate level that are accessible and promoted on academic department Web sites in addition to the library's site.
- Partnering with writing programs and centers to develop, publicize, and disseminate training materials for graduate students who teach writing to undergraduates, and to collaborate on training sessions for graduate students.

NIH says that to be effective, ethics training programs should be interactive and compulsory, should last throughout graduate school, and include "broad-based participation by faculty and administration" as well as "outside speakers" and activities that reinforce training (Bird, 1998, p.179). In other words, efficacy depends on a committed, multi-pronged approach. If partnerships across campus are an element of such an approach, then the players would naturally include faculty and librarians, as well as deans and writing programs. Deans are interested in reducing and preventing academic integrity violations and training transgressors. Writing programs are the front lines for teaching writing skills, including in many cases avoidance of plagiarism, and many programs use graduate students as writing instructors. Collaborations between all these interested groups can increase opportunities and settings for student learning and provide various instructor perspectives. The potential impact of collaborative efforts is greater than each group could achieve on its own.

Areas for further research that could assist librarians seeking to expand their role in the area of graduate student academic integrity training include:

- An assessment of the long-term effectiveness of various pedagogical techniques and tools;
- A survey of approaches for successful collaboration of librarians with faculty, deans, and writing programs;

- An evaluation of one or more such collaborations in terms of viability and effectiveness in the short and long term;
- A survey of graduate students who teach in writing programs to discover whether they teach undergraduates about plagiarism and what kind of training they receive in order to do so.[2]

Studies like these could provide methods to assess the effectiveness of programs, offer new ideas, and further the cause of cross-campus collaborations in service of a common goal. Librarians who work with graduate students have a great deal to offer and much to gain by viewing academic integrity as part of information literacy and becoming part of the solution to a widespread set of problems across many disciplines. This endeavor can provide an opportunity to contribute both to the ethical education of future doctors, lawyers, scientists, writers, psychologists, and businesspeople and to the honesty of the scholarly record they leave behind.

NOTES

1. The article databases searched for this survey were: America: History and Life, AnthroPlus, ATLA Religion, Business Source Premier, ComAbstracts (CIOS), Criminal Justice Abstracts, EconLit, Education Full Text, ERIC, Essay & General Literature Index, Expanded Academic ASAP ("peer-reviewed"), Francis, GeoRef, Hein Online, Inspec, LexisNexis Academic (Law Reviews), Library Literature & Information Science Full Text, LISA (Library & Information Science Abstracts), LLBA (Linguistics and Language Behavior Abstracts), MLA International Bibliography, PAIS International, Philosopher's Index, PsycINFO, PubMed, Social Services Abstracts, Sociological Abstracts, Web of Knowledge (Social Sciences Citation Index, Arts & Humanities Citation Index, Science Citation Index), and Worldwide Political Science Abstracts. I also searched the UCLA Library Catalog and WorldCat.

2. To investigate the literature on writing programs, I searched ERIC, the MLA International Bibliography, and LISA. Although some writing programs use graduate student instructors, the literature on this discusses their role as program administrators or teachers but does not mention how or whether they teach about plagiarism.

REFERENCES

Abasi, A. R., Akbari, N., & Graves, B. (2006). *Journal of Second Language Writing, 15*, 102-117. Retrieved December 27, 2006, from ScienceDirect database.

Altman, E. (1997). The implications of research misconduct for libraries and librarians. In E. Altman & P. Hernon (Eds.), *Research misconduct: Issues, implications, and strategies* (pp. 113-123). Greenwich, CT: Ablex.

Anderson, M. S. (1996). Misconduct and departmental context: Evidence from the Acadia Institute's Graduate Education Project. *Journal of Information Ethics, 5*(1), 15-33.

Anderson, M. S. (2002). What would get you in trouble: Doctoral students' conceptions of science and its norms. In N. H. Steneck & M. D. Scheetz (Eds.), *Investigating research integrity: Proceedings of the first ORI Research Conference on Research Integrity, November 2000* (pp. 19-25): Office of Research Integrity, Department of Health and Human Services. Retrieved August 14, 2006 from http://ori.dhhs.gov/documents/ proceedings_rri.pdf.

Anderson, M. S., Louis, K. S., & Earle, J. (1999). Disciplinary and departmental effects on observations of faculty and graduate student misconduct. In J. M. Braxton (Ed.), *Perspectives on scholarly misconduct in the sciences* (pp. 213-235). Columbus: Ohio State University Press. [Originally published in *Journal of Higher Education*, 1994, 65(3), 331-350.]

Angélil-Carter, S. (2000). *Stolen language? Plagiarism in writing.* Harlow, Eng.: Longman.

Association of College and Research Libraries. (2000). *Information literacy competency standards for higher education.* Chicago: American Library Association. Retrieved September 8, 2006, from http://www.ala.org/ acrl/ilcomstan.html.

Auer, N. J., & Krupar, E. M. (2001). Mouse click plagiarism: The role of technology in plagiarism and the librarian's role in combating it. *Library Trends, 49*(3), 415-432.

Baggaley, J., & Spencer, B. (2005). The mind of a plagiarist. *Learning, Media & Technology, 30*(1), 55-62.

Baldwin, D. C., Jr., Daugherty, S. R., Rowley, B. D., & Schwarz, M. R. (1996). Cheating in medical school: A survey of second-year students at 31 schools. *Academic Medicine, 71*(3), 267-273.

Barks, D., & Watts, P. (2001). Textual borrowing strategies for graduate-level ESL writers. In D. Belcher & A. Hirvela (Eds.), *Linking literacies: Perspectives on L2 reading-writing connections* (pp. 246-267). Ann Arbor, MI: University of Michigan Press.

Bartlett, T., & Smallwood, S. (2004, December 17). Mentor vs. protégé. *The Chronicle of Higher Education 51*(17), A14-15. Retrieved June 16, 2006, from http://chronicle.com.

Bilge, A., Shugerman, R. P., & Robertson, W. O. (1998). Misrepresentation of authorship by applicants to pediatrics training programs. *Academic Medicine, 73*(5), 532-533.

Bird, S. J. (1999). Including ethics in graduate education in scientific research. In J. M. Braxton (Ed.), *Perspectives on scholarly misconduct in the sciences* (pp. 174-188). Columbus: Ohio State University Press.

Bloch, J. (2001). Plagiarism and the ESL student: From printed to electronic texts. In D. Belcher & A. Hirvela (Eds.), *Linking literacies: Perspectives on L2 reading-writing connections* (pp. 209-228). Ann Arbor, MI: University of Michigan Press.

Boden, D., & Carroll, J. (2006). Combating plagiarism through information literacy. *Library + Information Update, 5*(1-2), 40-41.

Brainard, J. (2006, November 10). Universities experiment with classes in scientific ethics. *The Chronicle of Higher Education 53*(12), A22. Retrieved December 19, 2006, from http://chronicle.com.

Branstetter, S. A., & Handelsman, M. M. (2000). Graduate teaching assistants: Ethical training, beliefs, and practices. *Ethics & Behavior, 10*(1), 27-50.

Brinkley, A., Dessants, B., Flamm, M., Fleming, C., Forcey, C., & Rothschild, E. (1999). Teaching as a graduate student. In *The Chicago handbook for teachers: A practical guide to the college classroom* (pp. 117-131). Chicago: University of Chicago Press.

Brown, B. S. (1995). The academic ethics of graduate business students: A survey. *Journal of Education for Business, 70*(3), 151-156.

Brown, S., & Kalichman, M. W. (1998). Effects of training in the responsible conduct of research: A survey of graduate students in experimental sciences. *Science and Engineering Ethics, 4*(4), 487-498.

Cabral-Cardoso, C. (2004). Ethical misconduct in the business school: A case of plagiarism that turned bitter. *Journal of Business Ethics, 49*, 75-89.

Caravello, P. S. (2006). Into the breach: Teaching graduate students to avoid plagiarism. In D. Cook & N. Cooper (Eds.), *Teaching information literacy skills to social sciences students and practitioners: A casebook of applications* (pp. 225-234). Chicago: Association of College and Research Libraries.

Chandrasoma, R., Thompson, C., & Pennycook, A. (2004). Beyond plagiarism: Transgressive and nontransgressive intertextuality. *Journal of Language, Identity, and Education 3*(3), 171-193.

Collins, M. E., & Amodeo, M. (2005). Responding to plagiarism in schools of social work: Considerations and recommendations. *Journal of Social Work Education, 41*(3), 527-543.

Dans, P. E. (1996). Personal and professional qualities of medical students. *Academic Medicine, 71*(1), S70-S72.

Decoo, W. (2002). *Crisis on campus: Confronting academic misconduct.* Cambridge, MA: MIT Press.

Elphinstone, L., & Schweitzer, R. (1998). *How to get a research degree: A survival guide.* St. Leonards, Australia: Allen & Unwin.

Ercegovac, Z., & Richardson, J. V., Jr. (2004). Academic dishonesty, plagiarism included, in the digital age: A literature review. *College & Research Libraries, 65*(4), 301-318.

Fishman, K. D. (1999). No free lunch: Did a Cornell nutritionist steal his student's meal ticket? *Lingua Franca, 9*(1), 42-51.

Fly, B. J., van Bark, W. P., Weinman, L., Kitchener, K. S., & Lang, P. R. (1997). Ethical transgressions of psychology graduate students: Critical incidents with implications for training. *Professional Psychology: Research and Practice, 28*(5), 492-495.

Gabbay, D. S. (1999). A medical student honor code. *Emergency Medicine Clinics of North America, 17*(2), 417-428. Retrieved August 19, 2006, from MDConsult database.

Gerdy, K. (2004). Law student plagiarism: Why it happens, where it's found, and how to find it. *Brigham Young University Education and Law Journal*, 431-440. Retrieved August 9, 2006, from LexisNexis Academic database.

Gerhardt, D. R. (2006). Plagiarism in cyberspace: Learning the rules of recycling content with a view towards nurturing academic trust in an electronic world. *Richmond*

Journal of Law & Technology, 12. Retrieved August 9, 2006, from LexisNexis Academic database.

Gorney, C. (2001). Getting it right. *American Journalism Review 23*(2), 28-29.

Hall, J. (2005). Plagiarism across the curriculum: How academic communities can meet the challenge of the undocumented writer. *Across the Disciplines: Interdisciplinary Perspectives on Language, Learning, and Academic Writing, 2.* Retrieved December 26, 2006, from http://wac.colostate.edu/atd/articles/hall2005.cfm.

Hamilton, D. (2003). Plagiarism: Librarians help provide new solutions to an old problem. *Searcher, 11*(4), 26-28.

Howard, R. M. (1999). *Standing in the shadow of giants: Plagiarists, authors, collaborators.* Stamford, CT: Ablex.

Howard, R. M. (2001, November 16). Forget about policing plagiarism: Just teach. *The Chronicle of Higher Education 48*(12), B24. Retrieved December 19, 2006, from http://chronicle.com.

Hsu, A. Y.-P. (2003). Patterns of plagiarism behavior in the ESL classroom and the effectiveness of instruction in appropriate use of sources (Doctoral dissertation, University of Illinois at Urbana-Champaign, 2003). *Dissertation Abstracts International 64A,* 833.

Jackson, P. A. (2006). Plagiarism instruction online: Assessing undergraduate students' ability to avoid plagiarism. *College & Research Libraries, 67*(5), 418-428.

Kennedy, D. (1997). To mentor. In *Academic duty* (pp. 97-116). Cambridge, MA: Harvard University Press.

Kerkvliet, J., & Sigmund, C. L. (1999). Can we control cheating in the classroom? *Journal of Economic Education, 30*(4), 331-343. Retrieved August 16, 2006, from JSTOR database.

Koerber, A., Botto, R. W., Pendleton, D. D., Albazzaz, M. B., Doshi, S. J., & Rinando, V. A. (2005). Enhancing ethical behavior: Views of students, administrators, and faculty. *Journal of Dental Education, 69*(2), 213-224.

Lampert, L. D. (2004). Integrating discipline-based anti-plagiarism instruction into the information literacy curriculum. *Reference Services Review, 32*(4), 347-355.

Langlais, P. J. (2006, January 13). Ethics for the next generation. *The Chronicle of Higher Education 52*(19), B11. Retrieved May 30, 2006, from http://chronicle.com

Lapsansky, E. J. (2004). An honor system for historians? *Journal of American History 90*(4). Retrieved December 19, 2006, from the History Cooperative database.

Lawson, A. E., Lewis, C. M., Jr., & Birk, J. P. (2000). Why do students "cook" data? *Journal of College Science Teaching, 29*(3), 191-198.

LeClercq, T. (1999a). Confusion and conflict about plagiarism in law schools and law practice. In L. Buranen & A. M. Roy (Eds.), *Perspectives on plagiarism and intellectual property in a postmodern world* (pp. 195-203). Albany: State University of New York Press.

LeClercq, T. (1999b). Failure to teach: Due process and law school plagiarism. *Journal of Legal Education, 49*(2), 236-255. Retrieved August 11, 2006, from HeinOnline database.

Legal Writing Institute. (2003). *Law school plagiarism v. proper attribution: A publication of the Legal Writing Institute.* Legal Writing Institute. Retrieved Sept. 5, 2006, from http://www.lwionline.org/publications/plagiarism/policy.pdf.

Lerman, L. G. (2001). Misattribution in legal scholarship: Plagiarism, ghostwriting, and authorship. *South Texas Law Review, 42.* Retrieved August 9, 2006, from LexisNexis Academic database.

Love, P. G., & Simmons, J. (1998). Factors influencing cheating and plagiarism among graduate students in a college of education. *College Student Journal, 32*(4), 539-550.

Martin, D. F. (2005). Plagiarism and technology: A tool for coping with plagiarism. *Journal of Education for Business, 80*(3), 149-152.

Mathur, R., & Offenbach, S. I. (2002). Preliminary observations on faculty and graduate student perceptions of questionable research conduct. In N. H. Steneck & M. D. Scheetz (Eds.), *Investigating research integrity: Proceedings of the first ORI Research Conference on Research Integrity, November 2000* (pp. 35-40). Washington, D.C.: Office of Research Integrity, Department of Health and Human Services. Retrieved August 14, 2006, from http://ori.dhhs.gov/documents/proceedings_rri.pdf.

McCabe, D. L. (2005). *CAI research release.* Center for Academic Integrity. Retrieved August 25, 2006, from http://www.academicintegrity.org/cai_research.asp.

McCabe, D. L., Butterfield, K. D., & Treviño, L. K. (2006). Academic dishonesty in graduate business programs: Prevalence, causes, and proposed action. *Academy of Management Learning & Education, 5*(3), 294-305.

McCabe, D. L., & Treviño, L. K. (1997). Individual and contextual influences on academic dishonesty: A multicampus investigation. *Research in Higher Education, 38*(3), 379-396.

McCabe, D. L., Treviño, L. K., & Butterfield, K. D. (2001). Cheating in academic institutions: A decade of research. *Ethics & Behavior, 11*(3), 219-232.

McCullough, M., & Holmberg, M. (2005). Using the Google search engine to detect word-for-word plagiarism in master's theses: A preliminary study. *College Student Journal, 39*(3), 435-441.

McSkimming, M. J., Sever, B., & King, R. S. (2000). The coverage of ethics in research methods textbooks. *Journal of Criminal Justice Education, 11*(1), 51-63.

Newman, I., & Waechter, D. (2000). *Examination of the factor structure of the cheating scale.* ERIC Document 447186.

Nonis, S., & Swift, C. O. (2001). An examination of the relationship between academic dishonesty and workplace dishonesty: A multicampus investigation. *Journal of Education for Business, 77*(2), 69-77.

Oberlander, S. E., & Barnett, J. E. (2005). Multiple relationships between graduate assistants and students: Ethical and practical considerations. *Ethics & Behavior, 15*(1), 49-63.

Online Ethics Center for Engineering and Science at Case Western Reserve University. (2005). *Onlineethics.org: Responsible research scenarios.* Retrieved September 11, 2006, from http://www.onlineethics.org/reseth/ scenarios.html.

Osborn, E. (2000). Punishment: A story for medical educators. *Academic Medicine, 75*(3), 241-244.

Parrish, D. M. (2004). Scientific misconduct and findings against graduate and medical students. *Science and Engineering Ethics, 10*(3), 483-491.

Penzel, W. R. (2000). Perceptions, attitudes, and rates of cheating in doctoral psychology and law students (Doctoral dissertation, Hofstra University, 2000). *Dissertation Abstracts International, 61,* 3266.

Prior, P. A. (1998a). Images of authorship in a sociology research team. In *Writing/Disciplinarity: A sociohistoric account of literate activity in the academy* (pp. 160-179). Mahwah, NJ: Lawrence Erlbaum Associates.

Prior, P. A. (1998b). Trajectories of participation: Two paths to the MA. In *Writing/Disciplinarity: A sociohistoric account of literate activity in the academy* (pp. 99-134). Mahwah, NJ: Lawrence Erlbaum Associates.

Reybold, L. E. (2002). Constructing a personal model of research: Academic culture and the development of professional identity in the professorate. In N. H. Steneck & M. D. Scheetz (Eds.), *Investigating research integrity: Proceedings of the first ORI Research Conference on Research Integrity, November 2000* (pp. 41-47). Washington, D.C.: Office of Research Integrity, Department of Health and Human Services. Retrieved August 14, 2006, from http://ori.dhhs.gov/documents/proceedings_rri.pdf.

Rinnert, C., & Kobayashi, H. (2005). Borrowing words and ideas: Insights from Japanese L1 writers. *Journal of Asian Pacific Communication, 15*(1), 31-56.

Robin, R. (2004). *Scandals and scoundrels: Seven cases that shook the academy.* Berkeley: University of California Press.

Rose, M. R., & Fischer, K. (1998). Do authorship policies impact students' judgments of perceived wrongdoing? *Ethics & Behavior, 8*(1), 59-79.

Rytting, J. H., & Schowen, R. L. (1998). Issues in scientific integrity: A practical course for graduate students in the chemical sciences. *Journal of Chemical Education, 75*(10), 1317-1320.

Sandler, J. C., & Russell, B. L. (2005). Faculty-student collaborations: Ethics and satisfaction in authorship credit. *Ethics & Behavior, 15*(1), 65-80.

Schrag, B., Ferrell, G., & Weil, V. (2003). Barking up the wrong tree? Industry funding of academic research: A case study with commentaries. *Science and Engineering Ethics, 9*(4), 569-582.

Sheard, J., & Dick, M. (2003). Influences on cheating practice of graduate students in IT courses: What are the factors? *SIGCSE Bulletin, 35*(3), 45-49.

Simmons, M. H. (2005). Librarians as disciplinary discourse mediators: Using genre theory to move toward critical information literacy. *portal: Libraries and the Academy, 5*(3), 297-311.

Swazey, J. P., Anderson, M. S., & Louis, K. S. (1993). Ethical problems in academic research: A survey of doctoral candidates and faculty raises important questions about the ethical environment of graduate education and research. *American Scientist, 81*, 542-553.

Tankersley, K. C. (1997). Academic integrity from a student's perspective. *Journal of Dental Education, 61*(8), 692-693.

Teplitsky, P. E. (2002). Perceptions of Canadian dental faculty and students about appropriate penalties for academic dishonesty. *Journal of Dental Education, 66*(4), 485-506.

Tryon, G. S. (2000). Ethical transgressions of school psychology graduate students: A critical incidents survey. *Ethics & Behavior, 10*(3), 271-279.

Tryon, G. S., Bishop, J., & Hatfield, T. A. (2002). *School psychology graduate students' beliefs about dissertation authorship credit.* ERIC Document 470012.

Turner, S. P., & Beemsterboer, P. L. (2003). Enhancing academic integrity: formulating effective honor codes. *Journal of Dental Education, 67*(10), 1122-1129.

Vacha-Haase, T. R. (1995). Impaired graduate students in APA-accredited clinical, counseling, and school psychology programs (Doctoral dissertation, Texas A&M University, 1995). *Dissertation Abstracts International 56A*, 3477.

Vesilind, P. A. (2000). Academic integrity. In *So you want to be a professor? A handbook for graduate students* (pp. 143-159). Thousand Oaks, CA: Sage Publications.

Wajda-Johnston, V. A. (2001). Academic dishonesty in graduate programs: Beliefs, perceptions and behavior of students, faculty and administrators (Doctoral dissertation, Saint Louis University, 2001). *Dissertation Abstracts International 62B*, 2507.

Wajda-Johnston, V. A., Handal, P. J., Brawer, P. A., & Fabricatore, A. N. (2001). Academic dishonesty at the graduate level. *Ethics & Behavior, 11*(3), 287-305.

Walters, L. R. (1997). Implications of misconduct for bibliographic instruction. In E. Altman & P. Hernon (Eds.), *Research misconduct: Issues, implications, and strategies* (pp. 101-112). Greenwich, CT: Ablex.

Wasley, P. (2006, August 11). The plagiarism hunter. *The Chronicle of Higher Education 52*(49), A8. Retrieved December 19, 2006, from http://chronicle.com.

Werner, D. L., Heiberger, M. H., Feldman, J., & Johnston, E. (2000). The prevalence of unethical student behavior in optometry schools. *Optometric Education, 25*(3), 82-87.

Whitley, B. E., Jr. (1998). Factors associated with cheating among college students: A review. *Research in Higher Education, 39*(3), 235-274.

Whitley, B. E., Jr., & Keith-Spiegel, P. (2001). Academic integrity as an institutional issue. *Ethics & Behavior, 11*(3), 325-342.

Wiener, J. (2005). Feminism and harassment: Elizabeth Fox-Genovese goes to court. In *Historians in trouble: Plagiarism, fraud, and politics in the ivory tower* (pp. 13-30). New York: New Press.

Wood, G. (2004). Academic original sin: Plagiarism, the Internet, and librarians. *Journal of Academic Librarianship, 30*(3), 237-242.

Yarbrough, M. V. (1996). Do as I say, not as I do: Mixed messages for law students. *Dickinson Law Review, 100*(3), 677-684. Retrieved August 9, 2006, from HeinOnline database.

Integrating Information Literacy into the Graduate Liberal Arts Curriculum: A Faculty-Librarian Collaborative Course Model

Judy Xiao
David Traboulay

A LIBRARIAN'S INITIATIVE

As an academic librarian and graduate of the Master of Arts in Liberal Studies program, I broached the idea of a teaching collaboration with Professor Traboulay who taught the concluding master's thesis seminar. I felt that the character of the course's method and content of interdisciplinary learning created wonderful opportunities for integrating information literacy into the course. Professor Traboulay was well aware of the "increasingly complex and expansive information universe" that was available (Raspa & Ward, 2000, p. 15), and the need for students to learn how to find, evaluate and use information effectively. The issue of plagiarism was worrisome to him and many faculty members confessed that the practice was widespread. I offered to teach his students how to use Chicago-style citation and the plagiarism detection service Turnitin to avoid plagiarism. He liked my assertion that we should seek a solution that was educational rather than punitive. I persuaded him that utilizing the Blackboard Learning System in his course would be an exciting addition to the Socratic teaching method he was accustomed to using. He was happy to accept my offer to collaborate with him with the expectation that I would be the resource person in teaching how to use Blackboard and Turnitin effectively.

The purpose of the course was to facilitate the writing of the master's theses of 20 students, and its architecture was designed around the interaction between faculty members and students, oral and written critiques of thesis proposals, chapters, and the final version of the thesis. In addition, the course included selected philosophical works for discussion as one way to encourage students to ground their theses topics to a liberal arts concept or question. The learning experience in this course was unique. With the spirit and methods of the philosopher Socrates, Professor Traboulay made students see that learning brought self-awareness and sympathy for others. As students made personal connections to their theses, their voices articulated insights about themselves and the world that many students did not think that they were capable of finding (Ward, 2006).

My role in our collaboration confirmed my own view that what we do as librarians is a vital and essential component of the liberal arts

(Shapiro & Hughes, 1996). As I helped students to search for scholarly materials and encouraged them to critique their sources, it made me aware that the training and skills of a librarian prepared me for the key value that integrates the liberal arts, namely, the search for the truth of a question. Librarians have a great deal to offer in assisting students in this process. By working closely with our colleagues across campus, building strong relationships with our students, and actively engaging in our own learning, we can achieve the highest aspirations of information literacy–"to help students become transformed so that they might transform the world" (Ward, 2006, p. 402).

THE PERSPECTIVE OF AN HISTORIAN

We have chosen to reflect and write about the usefulness of collaboration in a graduate course. While we have a broad experience of the difficulties of undergraduate teaching that prevail at most public urban universities and colleges, we feel that good teaching is important at the graduate level as well. Graduate students generally do not bring the same basic problems as undergraduates, but we have found that we cannot expect them to reach the level of maturity and sophistication in their journey to knowledge and wisdom on their own. The purpose of this article is to open further the window on graduate learning and to argue that, not only does education at the graduate level require excellent teaching, but also that collaborative teaching is one of the effective ways of improving learning. Although we emphasize the virtue of collaboration between librarian and historian as the major reason for the success of the class, we must mention the significance of using the Socratic method as the key to understanding how this course was taught.

Let me describe the Socratic method more fully because it is exceedingly difficult to master. It requires great patience in allowing students the time to articulate their views; there must be a willingness to risk departing from an original plan or question and to use students' insights as new roads to travel intellectually. One also has to develop the instinct to know when and how to revert to the original idea, if at all. At its best, this process allows students to see professors as vulnerable, not having all the answers, open and respectful of their ideas. This method enhances the mutual respect between students and teachers. Equally important, it allows students to observe how much we love knowledge for its own sake, a lesson we absolutely must communicate to students whose world is essentially about using knowledge primarily as an instrument.

THE MA IN LIBERAL STUDIES PROGRAM

The Master of Arts in Liberal Studies (MALS) program at College of Staten Island, the City University of New York (CUNY) is open to all qualified holders of a bachelor's degree. It is designed to provide students the opportunity to study critically modern Western society, culture, and thought by intensive examination of central works and topics in the liberal arts and by comparison with other societies and cultures. The major focus of the curriculum is on the social sciences and humanities with attention paid to the impact of science and technology. There are seven core courses, two electives, and a master's thesis.

WORKSHOP SEMINAR ON THE THESIS

Each student chooses a thesis topic in consultation with the director of the program during the final school semester. A faculty supervisor is selected for each student on the basis of appropriate expertise. The student is expected to meet with his or her faculty supervisor at least six times during the semester and record their discussions in a journal. Six years ago, general dissatisfaction with the quality of the master's essay led us to change the requirement to a thesis with the expectation that a thesis would require greater research and a larger body of writing. At the same time we wanted to preserve the idea that the thesis must be linked to liberal arts themes, theories, and events discussed in our curriculum. This course was a workshop on the thesis where students gave periodic presentations on the progress of their study and received critique from the instructor and fellow students.

Students were assigned Edward W. Said's (1996) *Representations of the Intellectual* for initial discussions during the first three weeks of classes. This work is a discussion of the rights and obligations of a scholar/intellectual. It was important to discuss the ideal virtues and values that underpinned our Liberal Studies Program. We then discussed the thesis proposals and offered critiques. Students were expected to be familiar with each other's proposal given at the beginning of the course. For the final segment, each student presented the completed version of one chapter of his or her thesis.

THE INFORMATION LITERACY COMPONENT

Professor Traboulay and I worked together to design an information literacy component that would be seamlessly integrated into the course. Our goal was to teach students effective research skills so that they could complete their thesis. We wanted students to have the ability to successfully define a topic, to locate, evaluate, and use information effectively. At the same time, we wanted them to be actively engaged in the research process and to touch the world through their research questions. Effective strategies were implemented to help achieve our objectives. A description and discussion of the main components follows.

The Blackboard Course Web site

We developed a Blackboard course Web site to support the traditional course and library instruction. Course syllabus, course documents, library instruction components, and course-related library resources were all placed on the course Web site so that students could access them from anywhere, at any time. We asked the students to post their questions, thesis proposals, chapters, and completed works on the discussion boards. Blackboard was new for many students in the class, and some acknowledged that they did not have the basic technology skills. We taught students how to use the many useful features and functions of Blackboard, and helped them become technology literate. Considering the wide variety of student exposures to technologies, we used various approaches to reach out to students, helping them in the classroom, on the Web, over the phone, and one-on-one in our offices. After a semester of hard work, many students gained the knowledge and skills necessary to take full advantage of new information resources and technologies. In evaluating the course, students commented on the effective use of Blackboard in the course, and how the integration of technology helped to enhance the learning process. Comments from two of the students follow:

> Blackboard allows students and professors to continue the learning experience outside of the classroom. Although the presentation of my proposal was during the last five minutes of class and there was no time for anyone to give me suggestions and recommendations during the class, I received a lot of information on Web sites and articles from my classmates through Blackboard. Additionally, I have seen how the incorporation of technology with education facilitates the need of students and faculty to develop relationships with one another

and assist with the learning process by making personal contributions to each other that they might not have been able to make during the class. Further more, I found the links to the library and information on how to write a thesis extremely useful. I would strongly recommend this method of instruction to any professor in a graduate program.

I agree with my classmates in that our class got to know one another a lot better after we started posting on Blackboard this term, in addition to learning more about each other's thesis topics. I am a little late in contributing because I had so much trouble signing on, but I have caught up and I have read everyone's chapters and have gained a lot of knowledge about a lot of subjects I didn't possess before. It's a little like living in the19th century when serial novels were in vogue and people had to wait for the monthly chapters of the novel they were reading to be published. Blackboard has made sharing information a lot easier, in that we could access it when it was convenient for each of us. It's a great teaching tool.

Incorporating Blackboard into the course provided new opportunities and richer learning experiences for both students and instructors. However, our experience tells us that improved learning outcomes through technology require great effort and engagement from both instructors and students. We must be willing to learn, and to take risks.

Bring Library Resources to the Students

As the Internet becomes ubiquitous, students choose less and less often to use the library. Many ignore the high-quality library resources in favor of the Internet sources for their research needs. An OCLC report, *College Students' Perceptions of Libraries and Information Resources*, indicated that "89% of college students' information searches begin with a search engine" (OCLC, 2006). How can librarians and faculty persuade students to use the library resources? One of our strategies is to develop course-related library resources, integrate them into the faculty member's course Web site, and teach students to use these resources effectively. For this class, we created various resource pages, each of which focused on a specific topic containing hyperlinked library resources, including Finding Books in Library Catalogs, Finding Articles in Library Databases, Avoiding Plagiarism, and Chicago Style and Citing Your Sources. These resources were integrated into the course Web site, and students were able to access them conveniently just by clicking on the Library Resources link on the course menu (see Appendix A for a sample page). Many commented on how convenient it was to be able to access the library resources this way.

It is important to make library resources easy to use and readily available to maximize their use. A report on the use and users of electronic library resources published by the Council on Library and Information Resources concluded that "both faculty and students use and like electronic resources and most readily adopt them if the sources are perceived as convenient, relevant, and time saving to their natural workflow" (Tenopir, Hitchcook, & Pillow, 2003, p. iv). Discussions on the strategic importance of a library presence in faculty members' course Web sites also appeared in the literature (Cohen, 2002; Shank et al., 2003; Rieger et al., 2004). Shank and Dewald cautioned that "libraries risk being bypassed by this technology and losing relevance to students and faculty if they do not establish their presence in courseware" (p. 38). A research study at Cornell University Library confirmed the crucial importance of seamless linking of course Web sites and library resources "in an age where a growing number of students do not see a difference between what is offered by library resources and Web search engines" (Rieger et al., 2004, p. 205). And our experience tells us that convenience does not in itself lead to effective and increased use of library resources by students. We must teach students how to use these resources effectively, engage them in the research process, and be available to help them at their point of need.

Library Instruction

A library instruction session was held at the beginning of the semester to introduce students to the Blackboard course Web site and related library resources. The students logged on to Blackboard and were introduced to course-related library resources and shown how to search a database for articles. The students were given time to research their own topics, ask questions or explore the course Web site. The students were told that assistance would be available to them throughout the course, and they were encouraged to post questions to the *Library Resources* discussion forum.

To make library instruction effective, we decided to adopt a more personal and collaborative teaching approach. On the day of the scheduled library instruction, we designed an activity that asked each student to post his or her thesis proposal on Blackboard, and to come up with a list of key words or subject terms that described the main idea of his or her thesis. This learning activity proved to be very helpful. It provided students with opportunities not only to think critically about their research topics, their strategies when searching library catalogs and databases, but also to ask questions and seek help.

Library instruction continued with students posting their thesis proposals on Blackboard, and seeking help for information sources for their specific topics. Through discussion boards, e-mail, and one-on-one consultation, we answered students' questions, and guided them in locating articles and books relevant to their research questions. The online discussion forums became learning communities where the students, professor and librarian came together to exchange ideas, raise questions and help each other.

Integrating library instruction into the course and utilizing Blackboard for library instruction allowed me to overcome the time constraints of the "one-shot" library instruction session, to have more interaction with the students, and to help them at their point of need. For example, during the first face-to-face library session, due to limited class time, I was only able to demonstrate a multi-disciplinary database, *Academic Search Premier*, to teach students how to search for articles. Utilizing the *Library Resources* discussion forum, I was able to continue from where I left off, and guide students to the discipline-specific databases that were more useful for their specific needs. Guides to subject databases in education, health, literature, and history were sent to students via the discussion forum, with recommendations for books and articles on specific topics. To effectively help the students, Prof. Traboulay and I met twice a week to discuss progress of the students. I also served as the faculty thesis supervisor for one of the students in the class. The interaction with the students and the professor, and the exchange of thoughts and ideas was wonderful. Their perspectives on different subjects not only gave me an increased understanding of those subjects, but also inspired me to delve deeper into those subject areas so that I could help them better.

Dane Ward, Associate Dean for Public Services at Milner Library, Illinois State University, is a strong advocate for teaching information literacy that can make a difference in our students' lives and improve the world (Ward, 2001). He believes that "information literacy is a broader capacity than our current practices would suggest. In addition to critical thinking, information literacy includes information processes that explicitly address meaning, motivation, and the quality of life" (Ward, 2006, p. 396). It is important that we teach students how to find and evaluate information, but we must also find time to understand our students, to engage them with real world problems, and to help them better understand themselves and the world (Ward, 2006). As educators, we must embrace this broad notion of information literacy.

Preventing Plagiarism

Plagiarism by students is a growing concern on college campuses. A study conducted by Rutgers University Professor Donald McCabe points to a rise in plagiarism, with 70% of students admitting to some cheating, and nearly 40% admitting to plagiarizing using information cut and pasted from the Internet (Center for Academic Integrity, 2005). Librarians are in a unique position to form effective partnerships with faculty to educate students as to what constitutes plagiarism, why it is wrong, and how to avoid it (Lampert, 2004; Wood, 2004).

Like many faculty members, Professor Traboulay is disturbed by the increasing instances of plagiarism. He accepted my offer to work with him to educate his students about plagiarism and to help them avoid plagiarism. To be most effective, we decided not to schedule a one-shot plagiarism instruction session in the library, but to work closely together to integrate anti-plagiarism instruction into the course, and to help students better understand the issue of plagiarism as they work through their thesis. Our strategies included providing self-paced plagiarism prevention instruction materials for students; discussing the issue of academic honesty and plagiarism with students in and outside of class; and using Turnitin as a tool to teach students how to work with sources. Each of these efforts played a role in our success in preventing student plagiarism, but the most important factor of all was that we were there for the students as their mentors and co-learners throughout the research and writing of their theses.

We developed an online resource page titled *Avoiding Plagiarism* (see Appendix B) and made it available on the course Web site. Students were given this as an assignment to study, and asked to bring any questions or concerns to the class. We discussed the university's policy on academic integrity with the students, the serious consequences of committing plagiarism, and the importance of learning how to avoid it. The resources and discussions helped students understand what constitutes plagiarism, and the "how" and "why" behind the attribution of sources. We also spent time explaining our decision to use Turnitin to gain students' cooperation, making sure that they understand our intention of using Turnitin to help them avoid plagiarism, not to catch them.

Professor Traboulay told the students that I would be the resource person for Turnitin and encouraged them to seek my help. Students were able to follow the step-by-step instructions we provided to register with Turnitin, and submit their assignments. They first submitted one chapter of their thesis, and later their final completed thesis to Turnitin.

Turnitin produces an originality report after a article is submitted. This report provides the instructor and the student a summary of the matching text found in the student article. We distributed tip sheets to help students understand the report and taught them how to use the direct source comparison method to quickly compare highlighted matching text to its source to make sure that they had cited their sources correctly. We made ourselves available to students to help them and answer their questions. Students posted questions on Blackboard, called by phone, sent e-mails, and made office visits.

The overall percentage of matching text reported by Turnitin was less than 5% for the class. Students used the originality report to help them identify and correct the problems related to citation and paraphrasing. There was one student, however, whose first submission of one chapter was reporting 28% of matching text. We carefully examined both the Turnitin originality report and the student submission, making note of the problems in her article. We also found that several matching text reports were due to Turnitin's failure to exclude properly attributed quotations from suspect sources. The student was advised to first try correcting the problems herself with the aid of the Turnitin report. Later, we met with her to discuss her work, and helped her with any difficulties she had with paraphrasing and citing her sources. She learned from the process and did very well on her final thesis.

Using Turnitin successfully requires careful preparation and planning on the part of the instructor. It is most effective when used to teach students correct uses of sources rather than being used for the purpose of detection and punishment. Some instructors choose to submit students' work to Turnitin without involving the students, while others let students submit their work, but do not allow them to view the originality report. Literature on Turnitin typically focuses on its usefulness in helping faculty catch guilty students or its deterring effect on student plagiarism. We believe the real value of using Turnitin lies in actively involving students in the process, allowing them equal access to the originality report, and teaching them how to work with sources creatively and ethically using examples of plagiarism from students' work detected by Turnitin. The feedback from our students indicated that it was having access to the originality report, and getting feedback and help from the instructor and the librarian on their submitted work that made Turnitin a useful tool. Sheridan, Hitchcock, and Pillow (2005) reported that students wanted a copy of the originality report, and more feedback from instructors on the report so that they could see how well they did, how good their efforts were, and what was considered plagiarism (p. 245).

Dr. Howard, director of the writing program at Syracuse University, is a strong opponent of using software for detection and punishment. He firmly believes that good teaching is the key to preventing plagiarism, and calls on educators to examine their pedagogy, to write authentic assignments for students, and to spend more time helping students while they draft those papers (Howard, 2001). We share his convictions and hope that more librarians and classroom faculty will explore Turnitin's potential as an educational tool and move beyond the plagiarism detective mode to "become mentors of their students, not their enemies" (Howard, 2001, p. 2). As Professor Howard (2003) reminds us: "with information arriving as a cacophony of electronic voices, even well-intentioned students have difficulty keeping track of–much less citing–who said what" (p. 789).

EVALUATING THE COURSE

How can one evaluate whether a class was successful or not? Generally accepted criteria are an improved knowledge of the course content, development of analytical and writing skills, and the growth in confidence of students as individuals and collectively as a class. We tried to achieve a method between the claims of authority as teachers and enlarging the opportunities of freedom for students in the process of learning, restating often at critical moments the requirement of responsibility and discipline of both teacher and student. The ideal remains the development towards enlightenment and responsible freedom. In an interdisciplinary program such as our MALS program where students hold undergraduate degrees in a variety of disciplines and professors are encouraged to teach the core courses using the methodology of many disciplines, the process of learning is more complex than the traditional discipline-oriented method.

The graduating class in this course under review comprised twenty students, the largest in our history. Fourteen of our students graduated at the end of their second academic year, as we hoped they would. The remaining students were at different stages of completion. One should not make much of this statistic because it does not tell the whole story. For example, the quality of entering students, the willingness of faculty to give considerable time to advise students, the expansive nature of some topics, and, most importantly, the difficulties that many of our students have in finding the time for study while holding a full-time job and raising a family are all good reasons why many of our students do not finish their thesis at the end of two years. The high percentage of completion is one indicator that the achievement of this graduating class was greater than normal.

The Voices of Students

The major purpose of this course was practical, and it must be judged on whether it helped students in writing their theses. From this perspective we thought that it was successful. Its other purpose was a critical examination of humanistic and liberal ideas and this was why the course was structured around Edward Said's (1996) *Representations of the Intellectual*. The expectation was that this was the best structure to inspire and give practical help in writing the thesis and also to pin their topics to liberal arts and humanistic themes. Thesis proposals, critiques, chapters, and completed theses were placed on Blackboard and students were encouraged to comment on them.

There are occasions when a narrative style illuminates more clearly an event than an analytical approach, especially in communicating how students viewed this course. We asked students to write a brief evaluation at the end of the course on the different features of the course and to place their comments on Blackboard, informing them that their views would be useful when the graduate committee of the college met to discuss changes and reforms of programs. The profile of our class showed that three fourths were women, half of whom received their undergraduate degree from our college. These women were returning to college after their children had grown, were seeking opportunities for better jobs, or simply wanted to participate again in the climate of college learning. There were four foreign students in the course, women from China, Italy, Liberia, and Pakistan. Six students were under 30 years of age, four over 60, and the remaining ten between those ages. Fifteen students received their undergraduate degree in the liberal arts disciplines of sociology, English, and history; three in Business, Nursing, and Physical Education; two were retirees. Four students were members of the staff of the City University of New York colleges; nine were secondary school teachers; two were librarians; one was an officer with the

New York Police Department; one was a nurse; the other three worked in administrative positions in New York.

The story of each student's experience is rich in insight and is testament to the transforming power of democratic learning. There is no greater joy for a teacher than observing the progressive development of a student's literary, intellectual, and technical ability. This class was the final seminar of the MA program for the students and it was our good fortune to be a part of the end stage of their journey. We have selected the story of a few students' experiences to serve as vignettes to illustrate the character and texture of the voices of our students as subjects of their own experience.[1]

The youngest student brought a unique experience to the class. A graduate from Indiana University, he took a leave of absence after the first year with Professor Traboulay's encouragement to study in Paris. When he returned to the program, Professor Traboulay persuaded him to share with his colleagues a long essay he wrote about his experience. His journal touched his colleagues because of the sincerity and honesty of his reflections on encountering a foreign language and culture, after which fellow students would look to him as one of their leaders. Students seemed to like the fact that Professor Traboulay was willing to surrender his authority to students who had superior knowledge on a particular issue. This was one more confirmation of the successful practice of giving encouragement to the voices and stories of students as worthy of discussion. On the significance of reading *Representations of the Intellectual*, his point of view was typical of all the students. He asserted that the book "crystallized a lot of feelings I had had but never expressed." Said inspired him and he felt that it would give support and courage to "anyone who feels that they want to speak up about something they think is wrong." He offered the view that Said's work was "an ideal culmination of the authors they had studied throughout the program." About the segments on students' proposals and chapters, not only did he find the topics interesting, but also he was able to find echoes of his own ideas in the proposals of others, reiterating a theme articulated by many students. His interaction with his colleagues became friendly and practical in that he began to share books, articles, and ideas with them. He said that what was unique about this class was that the interaction "brought everyone's personality to the foreground. . . .This class took the shape of the people in it, and the subjects and materials were direct reflections of the people in it." Confessing that he did not [in the past] really enjoy school, he praised the course and program for "the freedom to allow my curiosity to wander and explore, but with enough direction and control to keep it all within a greater context." His thesis topic was on examining U.S. Foreign Policy from the 1890s through the 20th century in the hope of finding a pattern to explain the 2003 war in Iraq. In his conversations before class, long e-mail messages, and comments on Blackboard, we saw his thoughtful and sensitive mind at work, ever searching for the complexity of the issue.

Another student was a librarian who has a master's degree in Library Science and a BA in Political Science. For her thesis on Staten Island politics, she read practically everything written about Staten Island, covered the scholarly literature on U.S. history, and interviewed almost all of the important politicians on Staten Island. In her lecture as representative of her MALS graduating class at commencement, she bravely posed to the audience that American culture had been undermined by the liaison between politicians and corporations. She cited Edward Said in reminding her audience of professors, students, and their parents of their responsibility "to question patriotic nationalism, corporate thinking, and any sense of class, race or gender privilege," and warned of the dangers of being "motivated by rewards and the ladder of career plans." On the segments dealing with discussion on proposals and a chapter of her thesis, she felt that listening to the different approaches of colleagues made her look at her own thesis differently. The discussions built camaraderie and friendship, and overcame the isolation characteristic of focusing on one's topic. On critical comments by professors, she was surprisingly unequivocal in asserting its usefulness. "[Critiques by professors] enabled me to grow as a person and helped bring focus because one can lose focus along the way and that's exactly why it is so important to get input from supervisors. Inasmuch as I was attempting to gather, rein in, and then comment on an overwhelming abundance of information, they sorted out my interpretations, advised on removing the superfluous and illuminating the precious insights." Returning to the question of what she learned in the process of researching and writing her thesis, the workshop and its discussions, she said that "studying the history of Western thought from a critical perspective is the best reminder that history is not merely a series of events but is about humanity's pursuit of ideal. . . . I savored the art, literature, and music courses, began to understand how our capitalist society evolved and at times was driven by greed at the expense of the health and welfare of its general population. . . . Reading and discussing the works of Aristotle and Plato had the most profound effect on my thinking. In conclusion, I would suggest that Prof. E. W. Said's *Representations of the Intellectual* be added as a preface to the program because his advice goes to the heart of the MALS program, namely, to develop one's intellect in the hope of becoming better and braver citizens who are 'willing to speak the truth to power.'

Each student's story of what they learned was precious and unique. One student, whose topic on Post-Menopausal Women and the Health Establishment at first made us question how she would relate her topic to a liberal arts question, extolled the friendship that she found taking the courses with the same cohort of students, and how her colleagues and professors helped her develop her thesis to the point that she was proud of her achievement. She said that she saw herself as an intellectual, as Said described her, taking risks to speak the truth, armed with "reason and honesty." Another saw her thesis on the History of Women Returning to College as "speaking up for the voiceless and the underrepresented." The entire class was moved by the dilemma of the student who in her analysis of the Women's Movement in Pakistan wondered whether the disclosure of unpleasant facts would add more damage to the image of Islam, and applauded when she said that she was strengthened by Said's description of an intellectual which became "her magic wand as a weapon to stay my fear and inhibition." Ideas that arose from discussions about texts and proposals helped many to find their key to unlocking the door to the questions they posed in their thesis. The student who did her thesis on Gangs as a Sub-culture successfully used the idea that to understand the different Other we must make "a journey in." She said that she began to make progress on her topic when she began to study them "as an insider than as an outsider."

The purpose of these vignettes is to give a picture of how interesting, thoughtful, unique, and humane this class became where all of us not only achieved much of what we set out to do, but also learned a great deal from each other. The joy we felt collectively as a class is an insufficiently recognized criterion of successful teaching, described movingly in lines from a lady's journal in the frontispiece of Michael Farrell's (1963) only novel, *Thy Tears Might Cease:*

If you and I by a tale
Some hours of wandering life beguile,
Thy tears might cease
And we shall cease to mind ourselves awhile.

Hopefully, this narrative about the methods used, the structure and history of the course, and the voices, though fleeting, of the students will communicate a sense that exciting learning was taking place, and that our class had become a learning community where the voices and stories of students and professors interacted with each other as equally precious.

REASONS FOR SUCCESS?

First, we give credit to the use of the Socratic method described early in this essay, a method which focused on discussion, questions, encouraging students to participate, listening to their voices and emphases, and having the confidence to use their interests as detours in the journey of the class to the prescribed goal. It seems a marvel that such an approach has endured and has proven to be "a magic wand," to use one student's metaphor for the search for knowledge that transforms us.

Collaboration between the faculty member and librarian was a vital feature and reason for its success. Using Blackboard as an instrument and, in a sense, as texts, meant that although our class met only one evening a week for two hours, in reality the class continued for several hours in addition every week, since it became an obligation to respond to every question of a student and to participate in every discussion. Openness was celebrated as a virtue. Proposals, critiques, chapters, and completed theses were all placed on Blackboard. Integrating information literacy and plagiarism prevention instruction into the course helped improve the quality of student work, and prevented plagiarism. Our approach to Turnitin succeeded in helping us resolve problems when they first arose and overcome our fears about cheating.

Final reflection on why this course was a successful learning experience points to greater interaction among the students, the professor and the librarian. To use a word with philosophical association, there was greater "engagement" in terms of increasing time and opportunities for discussion, a deeper interest and meditation on students' work, a more active role in encouraging them, even nudging them that they had the mind and heart to succeed. One concrete example of this disposition was the offer to read their drafts of whatever they wrote, an offer that all the students accepted. The truth is that many students have little confidence in their ability to write well, especially a thesis of about fifty pages. They were immensely grateful when they read how much better the revised version was. We have no doubt that the success of this class was due in large part to the great amount of time we spent on the variety of initiatives we put in place.

NOTE

1. Permission has been received from the students of this class to use and quote from their evaluations of the course and their other writings in the course.

REFERENCES

Center for Academic Integrity (2005). Center for Academic Integrity (CAI) Research. Available at: http://www.academicintegrity.org/cai_research.asp.

Cohen, D. (2002). Course-Management Software: Where's the Library? *Educause Review*, May/June, 12-13.

Farrell, M. (1963). *Thy Tears Might Cease*. London: Arrow Books.

Howard, R. M. (2001). Forget About Policing Plagiarism. Just Teach. Available at: http://chronicle.com/prm/weekly/v48/i12/12b02401.htm.

Howard, R. M. (2003). Should Educators Use Commercial Services to Combat Plagiarism? No. *CQ Researcher*, 13(32), September 19, 2003, 789.

Lampert, L. (2004). Integrating Discipline-Based Anti-Plagiarism Instruction into the Information Literacy Curriculum. *Reference Services Review*, 32(4), 347-355.

OCLC (2006). College Students' Perceptions of Libraries and Information Resources. Available at: http://www.libraryjournal.com/clear/CA6340281.html.

Raspa, D. & Ward, D. (2000). Listening for Collaboration: Faculty and Librarians Working Together. In Dick Raspa and Dane Ward (Eds.), *The Collaborative Imperative: Librarians and Faculty Working Together in the Information Universe* (pp. 1-18). Chicago: Association of College and Research Libraries.

Rieger, O.Y., Horne, A.K., & Revels, I. (2004). Linking Course Web Sites to Library Collections. *The Journal of Academic Librarianship*, 30(3), 205-211.

Said, E.W. (1996). *Representations of the Intellectual: the 1993 Reith Lectures*. New York : Vintage Books.

Shank, J. & Dewald, N. (2003). Establishing Our Presence in Courseware: Adding Library Services to the Virtual Classroom. *Information Technology and Libraries*, 22(1), 38-43.

Shapiro, J. J. & Hughes, S. K. (1996). Information Technology as a Liberal Art. *Educom Review*, 31(2), 31-35.

Sheridan, J., Alany, R., & Brake, D. (2005). Pharmacy Students' Views and Experiences of Turnitin–an Online Tool for Detecting Academic Dishonesty. *Pharmacy Education*, 5(3/4), 241-250.

Tenopir, C., Hitchcook, B., & Pillow, A. (2003). *Use and Users of Electronic Library Resources: An Overview and Analysis of Recent Research Studies.* Washington, DC: Council on Library and Information Resources. Available at: http://www.clir.org/pubs/reports/pub120/pub120.pdf.

Ward, D. (2006). Revisioning Information Literacy for Lifelong Meaning. *The Journal of Academic Librarianship, 32*(4), 396-402.

Ward, D. (2001). The Future of Information Literacy: Transforming the World. *C&RL News,* 922-925.

Wood, G. (2004). Academic Original Sin: Plagiarism, the Internet, and Librarians. *The Journal of Academic Librarianship, 30*(3), 237-242.

APPENDIX A

This is an example of a Library Resources page accessible from within the course Web site. Library Resources and Turnitin are added to the course menu for easy access.

Quick Links to Library Resources and Services

1. CSI Library Home Page
2. Find Articles in Library Databases
3. Find Books in CUNY+ Catalog | WorldCat
4. Find Graduate Theses in the Library Catalog
5. Interlibrary Loan: Request for Books | Request for Articles
6. Guidelines for Submitting Your Master's Thesis to the Library
7. Library Hours and Phone Numbers to Know:
   Reference Desk: 718-982-4014; Interlibrary Loan: 718-982-4014
   Archives & Special Collections: 718-982-4128

Resources on the Internet

- Search Google
- Evaluating Web Sites: Criteria and Tools
- Turnitin Research Resources for Students

APPENDIX B

This is the content of the resource page titled Avoiding Plagiarism, available to students by clicking on the link Turnitin on the Blackboard course menu.

AVOIDING PLAGIARISM

Resources for Avoiding Plagiarism

1. Please read CUNY Policy on Academic Integrity (http://www1. cuny.edu/portal_ur/content/2004/policies/policies.html). You will find definitions and examples of academic dishonesty, including plagiarism and internet plagiarism.
2. Study style manuals to avoid plagiarism. To help you with your thesis, you may want to have a copy of the *A Pocket Style Manual*, fourth edition, by Diana Hacker. The author has a Student Companion Web site (http://dianahacker.com/pocket/) for the book, where you'll find guidelines and tips for documenting sources in Chicago style, exercises for integrating quotations and documenting sources, as well as annotated student sample article in Chicago style. You may also want to consult *The Chicago Manual of Style* (15th edition). The library has multiple copies of this title, available on reserve, in the reference collection and at the reference desk. Call No: Z253.U69 2003.
3. Take this interactive Research Exercises for Chicago Style (http://dianahacker.com/pocket/rs_menu.asp) developed by Diana Hacker to learn how to use sources correctly to avoid plagiarism, including recognizing common knowledge and integrating quotations in your thesis.
4. Turnitin Research Resources (http://www.turnitin.com/research_ site/e_home.html) defines plagiarism in easy-to-understand terms, provides tips on how to avoid plagiarism, as well as guidelines for proper citation using Chicago Style.

Turnitin

What Is Turnitin and How It Works for LBS 770?

Turnitin is an online plagiarism prevention and detection system that College of Staten Island has a subscription for its faculty and students. Every article submitted to this service is returned with a customized Originality Report, which shows you the results of

Turnitin's comparison of your work to content on the Web, to student papers previously submitted to Turnitin, and commercial databases of journal articles and periodicals.

In LBS 770, our intention to use Turnitin is to help you avoid plagiarism. You'll have the opportunity to submit your first assignment (one chapter of your thesis) to Turnitin, get an originality report, and check Turnitin's findings against your writing to make sure that you have cited sources correctly. This gives you opportunity to practice using this tool, and enables you to recognize plagiarism that may be unintentional so that you can make the necessary corrections. After that, you are required to submit your final thesis to Turnitin, and that's your 2nd assignment.

How Do I Get Started?

Follow the steps outlined below to register with Turnitin, create a user profile, and submit your first assignment (one chapter of your thesis) as required. If you encounter difficulty, post your questions on the course Web site, or let me and Prof. Traboulay know. I can arrange a short instruction session to walk you through the process. The *Student Quickstart* tutorial link provided below is very helpful, too. Please print it out and use it to help yourself.

1: Go to www.turnitin.com
2: Click on the New Users at the top of the homepage.
3: Select student for user type.
4: Type class ID (distributed in class) in the Turnitin class ID box,

Type class password in the Turnitin class enrollment password box.

Now you have successfully joined the class. Follow the instructions to complete creating your profile. Once you finish, you will be logged in to Turnitin, and you can start submitting your first assignment (one chapter of your thesis). You can view all of Turnitin's user manuals and documentation at: http://www.turnitin.com/static/training.html.

The following are a few quick links to get you started:

- Student Quickstart in PDF format
- Student User Manual in PDF format
- Student Quickstart Video
- Student Originality Report Video

The Influence of Rare Book and Manuscript Repositories on Graduate Research in the Humanities: The Graduate Research Fellowship Program

Kathryn James

INTRODUCTION

How does the rare book and manuscript library influence graduate research in the humanities? Graduate research, like other forms of research, does not happen in a vacuum. Barrett (2005) has most recently examined the external influences recognized by humanities graduate students in the development of their research projects. In asking how graduate students encountered and decided on ideas for research projects, Barrett found that

> Among participants, the three most common starting points for MA and PhD thesis projects were coursework, supervisors, and recognition of "gaps" in the literature. Several participants could trace their initial project ideas back to graduate-level coursework seminars and presentations. A few participants mentioned project ideas emerging out of independent reading courses, and two mentioned ideas emerging out of doctoral-level reading courses designed to produce a dissertation prospectus. (p. 327)

Barrett's findings highlight the importance of social influences in shaping the research process, a conclusion which reinforces a broader argument for the importance of social capital in shaping research and research networks (Johnson, 2004). Austin (2002) emphasizes this in writing that "as socialization or a preparatory experience for the faculty career, the graduate experience is the crucial point in time to determine whether or not students are exposed to the types of skills and expectations likely to confront them on the job" (p. 96).

To Barrett's list of influences–coursework, supervisors, and perceived openings in the literature of the field–should be added the rare book and manuscript repository. Primary sources, in electronic and material form, are central to graduate research in the humanities. The availability of collections–both through electronic or printed cataloguing and through research access to the collections themselves–directly shapes the research topics pursued (or not pursued) by graduate students in the humanities. What is the involvement of the rare book and manuscript repository in this process? What part, if any, does the rare book and manuscript repository play in the intellectual and professional development of humanities graduate students?

One answer can be found in the research fellowship program, as a mechanism through which rare book libraries directly and indirectly influence the professional development and socialization of graduate students in the academic humanities. Based on a comparison of residential research fellowship programs at twenty-three rare book and manuscript repositories, this article argues that fellowship programs perform three important functions. First, fellowship programs not only highlight the particular items and collections held by rare book and manuscript repositories, but also reinforce the identity of these collections through the application process. In the case of graduate students, the fellowship program and its application process concentrate attention on the specific holdings of rare book libraries, offering an incentive to students to frame their topics around the contents of a particular archive or collection. Second, the fellowship process encourages graduate students to imagine possible relationships between their research projects and the holdings of particular rare book and manuscript repositories, framing their research around a particular set of primary sources. Third, research fellowship programs contribute to the development of a research community in which the rare book and manuscript repository plays a central role. For graduate students, the fellowship offers the opportunity to meet with researchers, academics, curators, and librarians across the boundaries of institution, discipline, and career stage. Unlike that encountered in the graduate department, the research community fostered by the fellowship program is one in which the rare book and manuscript repository plays the central role.

This article is not concerned with the mechanics of research fellowship programs. Instead, the article examines the graduate research fellowship as one process, in the span of academic careers in the humanities, in which humanities researchers and rare book and manuscript repositories come into contact with one another. Rare book libraries, like all academic libraries, have an impact on research fields which extends beyond the literature that graduate students and other researchers find in the catalogs, the databases, and the stacks. To understand how our constituents are influenced by academic libraries, during the critical and intellectually formative period of the PhD program, is to understand both the role played by academic libraries in this process and the possibilities presented by this role. Research fellowship programs offer one example of the complex interactions between humanities researchers, beginning with their experience as graduate students, and rare book and manuscript repositories. Through shaping graduate research and fostering the development of academic fields and research communities, the graduate research fellowship program reinforces the absolute centrality of the academic library–and the rare book and manuscript repository–to the research and intellectual community of the humanities.

OVERVIEW OF FELLOWSHIP PROGRAMS

This study focuses on a particular category of research funding: the residential research fellowship. Many residential research fellowships are restricted to scholars already holding the doctorate. A significant number, however, are open to graduate students, especially those who have completed their exams and been admitted to the dissertation stage of their program. Some fellowships are also open for application to students at the pre-doctoral level, before they have completed the requirements of their doctoral program to proceed to the thesis.

The residential research fellowship is a particular type of program, in which funding is provided to allow a scholar to travel to a repository to conduct his or her research in its collections over a particular period. Funding periods range from two weeks to a year, for short- or long-term programs. Short-term fellowships are usually for a one- to three-month period; long-term fellowships are usually for a nine- to twelve-month period.

Institutions offering collections-based, residential graduate fellowships range across three broad categories:

- National organizations such as the Smithsonian and the Library of Congress;
- Academic-affiliated libraries such as Harvard University's Houghton Library, the University of Virginia's Albert and Shirley Small Special Collections Library, or Yale University's Beinecke Rare Book and Manuscript Library;
- Independent libraries, such as the American Philosophical Society, the Newberry Library, the Huntington Library or the Getty Research Institute.

This encompasses a spectrum of organizations, with widely different collections, missions, audiences, and sources of funding. To the graduate student, however, these institutions hold in common two key organizing characteristics: they offer money for graduate research in the humanities, and they have research collections upon which this fellowship research must be based.

What is the appeal of these programs to humanities graduate students or rare book libraries? That both participants in the fellowship program–the repository and the recipient–place a premium on the process can be demonstrated quite simply by the prevalence of residential research fellowships. Libraries, institutions, and professional societies together offer hundreds of research fellowships, to professional practitioners, graduate students, and independent scholars. On any given day, there are dozens if not hundreds of active announcements for grant funding and research fellowships to be found on H-Net, the Humanities and Social Sciences On-Line (today, as an example, there are 116). Many of these advertisements are topic- or field-specific; many are limited to post-doctoral researchers; many, however, are either directed towards doctoral candidates or are open to doctoral candidates, to compete for funding with post-doctoral and other researchers in the field.

For graduate students, the research fellowship is an important tool for professional development, as well as a straightforward opportunity for doctoral research in a particular collection. A visit to the "CV Doctor" at the Web site of the Chronicle of Higher Education will reveal the ubiquity of the "Awards and Honors" section of the humanities job candidate's curriculum vitae (Chronicle). Graduate fellowships act as an important gauge of the market value of humanities graduate students, in competing for scarce professional positions. A candidate's ability to attract funding for his or her research is an important marker of the candidate's research potential. Implicit in this equation is the assumption that candidates will be applying for research fellowships over the course of their graduate careers. Today's graduate fellow is tomorrow's post-doctoral or mid-career research fellow.

Collections Identity and the Applications Process

Fellowships frame the particular research collections of a rare book and manuscript library. Some institutions offer "named" fellowships, in which the donor of fellowship funding has specified either the category of recipient (graduate student, tenured faculty, independent researcher) or the focus of research (a particular collection or theme). Some institutions match the fellowship program to the holdings, offering fellowships which focus on distinct areas of the collections. An example of several named, topic- and collection-specific fellowships can be found in a selection of the Huntington Library's fellowships (Huntington Library):

- Francis Bacon Foundation Fellowships in Renaissance England
- Haynes Foundation Fellowships in Los Angeles History
- Reese Fellowship in American Bibliography and the History of the Book in the Americas
- Trent R. Dames Civil Engineering History Fellowship
- Christopher Isherwood Foundation Fellowship

Most fellowship programs are directed towards researchers with a need to use items specific to the repository's collections. An example can be found in the Newberry Library's fellowship description:

> Short-term fellowships are generally restricted to individuals from outside the metropolitan Chicago area and are primarily intended to assist researchers with a need to examine specific items in the Library's collection. (Newberry Library)

This requirement works to influence applicants to frame a research proposal around the holdings specific to a particular repository. In an age of the electronic ubiquity of particular copies of primary sources, the fellowship program has the unusual effect of fostering what Walter Benjamin termed the "aura" particular to individual, context-specific sources (Benjamin, 1968). One effect of the fellowship program, therefore, is to "brand" the library as the repository of certain unique items or collections. This is a significant aspect of the residential fellowship program, and one which becomes particularly visible during the fellowship application process.

The application process for residential fellowships exhibits several common characteristics across the range of repositories offering fellowship programs. Regardless of the type of fellowship (short- or long-term; specific to a collection or general), the applicant is required to submit a research proposal, outlining the significance of the project to the field and the particular relevance of the project to the library's collections. Other components of the application would be the inclusion of a curriculum

vitae, and the arrangement for one to three letters of reference supporting the candidate's application.

Across the board, however, repositories hosting research fellowships
emphasize the significance of the project proposal to the success of a
fellowship application. The project proposal comprises an essay, usually ranging in length from two to five pages, in which the candidate introduces the research project. The proposal is an opportunity for the
candidate to highlight the overall intellectual contribution to be made by
the project to a discipline and to emphasize the unique necessity of the
library's collections to the success of the research project. Dumbarton
Oaks offers a representative example of the criteria offered to the
candidate for the evaluation of fellowship proposals:

> Fellowships are awarded on the basis of (1) demonstrated schol-
> arly ability and preparation of the candidate (including knowledge
> of the requisite languages), (2) interest and value of the study or
> project, and (3) its relevance to the resources of Dumbarton Oaks.
> Award decisions are made by committees of scholars in the three
> fields. (Dumbarton Oaks)

The proposal sometimes requires candidates to frame a plan for his or
her research, and to offer an expected outcome, such as the completion
of a doctoral chapter or publication of an article. An example can be
found in the Newberry Library's instructions for the research proposal.
The application guide states that the project description is the most important aspect of the application:

> The project description is the most important part of the applica-
> tion. It should describe the project, explain its significance, de-
> scribe the Newberry materials to be consulted while you are in
> residence, and outline your plan of work. Short-term applicants
> should take special care to be as specific as possible about
> Newberry materials to be consulted during the proposed fellow-
> ship period. When appropriate, applicants should also make spe-
> cific reference to previous published scholarship that will be
> revised or supplanted by the proposed project. (Newberry Library)

Specificity–of the application to the collections, of the project to the
state of research in a given field–commands a premium in the evaluation of the fellowship application.

The research proposal has an important impact on graduate student
research. The project for a residential fellowship application must be

presented to the application board as being somehow uniquely suited to the strengths of a collection. The process of applying for a fellowship is one in which the applicant must convincingly demonstrate familiarity with the holdings–general or specific–of an institution. This is one point in the graduate student's career when he or she will encounter the rare book and manuscript repository's Web site, catalogs, and description of the collections. This is an important moment in the relationship between a graduate student and the particular library: if the student cannot find material relating to his or her project, he or she is unlikely either to make or to be successful in an application. The clarity of an institution's descriptions can affect who comes to research at the institution.

The fellowship application also maps out the professional network of a particular field. Fellowships might be advertised on popular general Web sites and list-servs, such as the Chronicle of Higher Education, H-Net, and Ex Libris. They might also be listed by societies and associations particular to more specific fields or specialties. Fellowship programs, in repeating the advertising and application process, with its regular deadlines, also become consistent features of the academic calendar. A graduate student might learn of a fellowship program through a range of sources, including those of the local information network of doctoral supervisor, instructors, library subject specialist, peers, or departmental bulletin board.

The fellowship program can be an opportunity for a library to develop its image in a field, continuing to foster graduate study based on specific collections or themes. It can also be an opportunity for an institution to change its reputation: a fellowship can encourage applicants in a new field, for which a repository might not be well-established as a resource, or encourage applicants to view an institution as a more prominent, useful, or friendly library in a particular field.

The research fellowship program helps to establish the identity and relevance of institutions within particular professional fields. Fellowships focus attention on particular collections, while the fellowship application process encourages applicants to imagine a convincing research project focused on that collection. This project, moreover, is usually required to convince a review panel of its significant contributions to a particular academic field. The implicit premise at work is that the collection is itself both worthy of researchers' attention and capable of supporting significant contributions to an academic field. This premise can be seen at work in the description of the requirements for the Library of Congress Kislak fellowship:

The Kislak Program supports scholarly research that contributes significantly to a greater understanding of the cultures and history of the Americas. It provides an opportunity for a period of up to four months of concentrated use of materials from the Kislak Collection and other collections of the Library of Congress, through full-time residency at the Library. (Library of Congress)

In writing a fellowship application–or, more likely, in the process of writing several fellowship applications for separate institutions–the graduate student becomes familiar with the holdings and "brands" of different rare book and manuscript repositories. He or she must also undergo the exercise of defining the relevance of a particular library's holdings to a project, or of creating a project for which these holdings would be relevant. There is, therefore, a relational process at work: the graduate student has to imagine a convincing relationship between a research project and a library's collections. The more convincing the relationship, the better the chance of acquiring research funding. As there is a vested incentive for graduate students to acquire funding, to enhance their research and employment prospects, the fellowship program can work to create continued interest in a repository's collections and to enhance its relevance to the professional practice of a discipline or field.

It is important to remember, however, that the rare book and manuscript repository has a different perspective on its identity and purpose than that held by a researcher, particularly a graduate student applying for a graduate research fellowship. To the graduate student, the rare book and manuscript repository is primarily the location of two specific, important, and potentially related resources: (1) funding for research, with the corresponding benefits for doctoral research and career prospects; (2) particular items or collections pertaining to doctoral research. Furthermore, the repository will always be only one repository among many which the student requires over the course of his or her research. The courtship ritual which the graduate fellowship applicant undertakes requires that he or she convince the host repository of the unique relevance of its resources to a particular project and, furthermore, of the importance of this project to the research in a particular field.

FELLOWSHIPS AND THE RESEARCH COMMUNITY

The idea of the research community is central to the residential research fellowship program. As resident fellows, graduate students have the opportunity to engage with scholars from different organizations, at varying stages of their careers. Participation in the life of an intellectual community–through sharing research, meeting new colleagues, participating in research seminars and colloquia–is a common requirement of fellowship programs, across institutional categories.

In some cases, the research community is quite explicitly determined by the fellowship program. Some institutions frame the fellowship program around a common annual theme, as in the example of the Center for Advanced Judaic Studies at the University of Pennsylvania, which is hosting its 2006 fellowship program around the theme of "Jewish and Other Imperial Cultures in Late Antiquity: Literary, Social, and Material Histories" (Center for Advanced Judaic Studies).

Others encourage the research community to develop more organically, by inviting fellows to participate in the research seminars, lectures, colloquia, and associated academic events. In fact, many fellowship programs require the fellow to participate in the intellectual life of the repository. An example can be found in the Getty Institute's program, which outlines the parameters of its fellowships as follows:

> Recipients are in residence at the Getty Research Institute, where they pursue research to complete their dissertations or to expand them for publication. Fellows make use of the Getty collections, join in a weekly meeting devoted to the annual theme, and participate in the intellectual life of the Getty Center. (Getty Institute)

The Getty is not alone in specifying the requirement to participate in the institutional research community, as can be seen in the example of the Colonial Williamsburg Foundation:

> Recipients are expected to be in continuous residence at the Library and to participate in the intellectual life of the Foundation's research and education campus. Fellows are invited also to attend colloquia, seminars, and lectures at the Omohundro Institute of Early American History and Culture and at the College of William and Mary. (Colonial Williamsburg Foundation)

The fellowship program frames a social network in which the rare book and manuscript repository plays an active central role in fostering the intellectual life of a research community. In addition, the graduate students and faculty at the host institution might also be involved in the social network underpinning the library's fellowship program. As the

Monticello description outlines, a research fellowship program can also work to create a network in which academics, curators, librarians, and researchers all participate in an intellectual community:

> Fellows are expected to be in residence at the Robert H. Smith International Center for Jefferson Studies, where they will have access to Monticello's expert staff and research holdings at the Jefferson Library as well as those of the University of Virginia. During their residencies, fellows are expected to deliver an informal 45-minute talk on their projects before an audience that typically consists of Monticello staff, University of Virginia faculty and students, and friends of the International Center. (Monticello)

The fellowship program can therefore hold an important social component, in mapping out an institutional or cross-institutional landscape of peers, colleagues, and potential employers.

The research fellowship program also allows the rare book and manuscript repository to frame an intellectual community around its own holdings. Graduate students will already have been familiar with their own departments and institutions, and might have begun to meet peers at graduate or professional conferences in their fields. The fellowship program, however, offers the graduate student the chance to spend time in a different academic community, one shaped by the repository and its collections rather than by the departmental politics of his or her home institution. The fellowship program, in effect, acts to "foster out" graduate students to different institutions and peer groups across the boundaries of discipline and career stage. Fellowships introduce new practitioners in the field to a broader interdisciplinary landscape of libraries, professionals, and fellow research fellows.

Finally, and not least, the fellowship allows the graduate student the opportunity of time to research and write in the context of a particular collection. This can have a lasting influence on the graduate student's research, and the topics which the graduate student undertakes for their doctoral or post-doctoral research.

CONCLUSIONS

Implications of Graduate Fellowships for Graduate Students

Research fellowships have a direct influence on the professional development and research interests of graduate students. Fellowships direct graduate students towards the particular collections of rare book and manuscript repositories, shaping their current and future research findings and interests. Fellowship funding is also an important mechanism for professional development, as graduate students prepare to compete on the market for academic employment. The fellowships offer important professional socialization opportunities, allowing graduate students to meet future colleagues from different institutions, at different stages of the professional career.

Implications of Graduate Fellowships for Rare Book and Manuscript Libraries

Graduate research fellowships also have a positive impact on rare book and manuscript repositories. Fellowships support the continued intellectual development of a field, encouraging new practitioners in original research through the use of primary source archives. Fellowships also work to emphasize the continued centrality of rare book and manuscript libraries to professional practice in the humanities.

The research fellowships can act to "brand" the repository's collections, giving the institution the opportunity to identify areas in which it holds collections of particular strength or interest, or research fields in which it can play a central role. Through providing funding for original research, rare book and manuscript libraries guarantee that their holdings continue to be relevant to discussion within an academic field and that these holdings are publicized, through citation, acknowledgement, or discussion. The annual fellowship application process therefore guarantees a consistent period of visibility for a repository and its collections in a given year. Graduate students will think about a particular repository with regard to their research. Referees, however, will also think about and engage with a particular library or collection, in the process of writing supporting letters of recommendation.

The fellowship program also fosters the repository's reputation throughout a broader academic community. The annual application process encourages new entrants into the profession to focus their research on the particular strengths of a repository's collections. On an annual basis, senior academics also encourage graduate students to apply for particular fellowships or write supporting letters of recommendation for applications.

The graduate fellowship program also enables the library staff of rare book and manuscript repositories to meet scholars at an early stage of their academic careers. The fellowship program creates an annual opportunity for the library to encounter the community of graduate fellowship applicants. The questions and confusions which arise from the fellowship application process can be a very useful source of information for a library, giving an external perspective on the strengths or weaknesses of the library's Web site, collections overview, and catalogs.

Implications of Graduate Fellowships for Rare Book and Manuscript Libraries

Communication with Graduate Researchers

The fellowship program is one opportunity for the repository to communicate directly with researchers, helping researchers to shape their projects and the repository's holdings, and supporting practitioners in their research. A graduate student can expect to research the fellowship programs, application processes, and collections of several rare book and manuscript repositories over the course of their graduate careers. As well as becoming an expert on a particular set of subjects, the graduate student must also begin to form an expertise in locating items within the collections of a variety of rare book and manuscript repositories. Each institution will have a different Web site, organized in different ways. Each institution will also vary in the extent of its on-line catalogs, the depth of information offered in its catalogs and finding aids, and the navigability of its electronic interfaces. This exploration of resources available across institutions provides new scholars with the opportunity-or challenge-to hone their information literacy skills, and for resident librarians to reinforce these skills in helping graduate student patrons.

Implications for Academic Libraries

Fellowships focus researchers' attention: the fellowship program is one means by which a rare book and manuscript library–and, by extension, its parent association or academic library–can focus graduate student and researcher attention on the particular strengths of the repository's collections. Fellowships therefore foster and perpetuate the research interest and impact of a repository's holdings, by helping to create a continual and continually new audience of researchers at work on the collections.

Fellowships focus library attention: the fellowship program is also one mechanism by which a repository can form a coherent idea of its own strengths. Putting a program into place involves asking self-examining questions, such as: Which are the collections which we think have the most research value–or which have value which has not yet been tapped by researchers? Which collections might encourage donor support, for the fund-raising or endowment of an individual fellowship? The fellowship program therefore offers a continual opportunity for the library to articulate its strengths as a research repository and to market these strengths to a broader audience of researchers, alumni, and potential donors.

REFERENCES

Austin, A.E. (2002). Preparing the Next Generation of Faculty: Graduate School as Socialization to the Academic Career. The Journal of Higher Education, 73 (1), 94-122.

Barrett, A. (2005). The Information-Seeking Habits of Graduate Student Researchers in the Humanities. Journal of Academic Librarianship, 31 (4), 324-331.

Benjamin, W. (1968). The Work of Art in the Age of Mechanical Reproduction. In H. Arendt (Ed.), Illuminations. London: Fontana.

Center for Advanced Judaic Studies, University of Pennsylvania. Web site: http://www.cjs.upenn.edu/.

The Chronicle of Higher Education. Web site: http://www.chronicle.org.

Colonial Williamsburg Foundation Fellowships and Internships. Web site: http://www.visitwilliamsburg.com/cw.htm.

Dumbarton Oaks Research Library and Collection. Web site: http://www.doaks.or.

Getty Research Institute. Web site: http://www.getty.edu/research/.

Humanities and Social Sciences On-line (H-Net). Web site: http://www.h-net.org.

Huntington Library. Web site: http://www.huntington.org/ResearchDiv/Fellowships.html.

Johnson, C. A. (2004). Choosing people: the role of Social Capital in Information Seeking Behaviour. Information Research, 10 (1).

Library of Congress. Web site: http://www.loc.gov/rr.

Monticello. Web site: http://www.monticello.org.

Newberry Library. Web site: http://www.newberry.org.

APPENDIX

Research Fellowship Programs Consulted

1. American Philosophical Society Library. Web site: http://www.amphilsoc.org.
2. Beinecke Rare Book and Manuscript Library, Yale University. Web site: http://www.library.yale.edu/beinecke.
3. Center for Advanced Judaic Studies, University of Pennsylvania. Web site: http://www.cjs.upenn.edu.
4. Colonial Williamsburg Foundation. Web site: http://www.visitwilliamsburg.com/colonial_williamsburg_foundation.htm.
5. Denver Public Library. Web site: http://www.denver.lib.co.us.
6. Dumbarton Oaks Research Library and Collection. Web site: http://www.doaks.org.
7. The Getty Research Institute. Web site: http://www.getty.org/research.
8. Gilder-Lehrman Institute of American History. Web site: http://www.gilderlehrman.org.
9. Harry Ransom Center for Research at the University of Texas at Austin. Web site: http://www.hrc.utexas.edu.
10. Houghton Library, Harvard College Library. Web site: http://hcl.harvard.edu/houghton.
11. The Huntington Library. Web site: http://www.huntington.org.
12. John Carter Brown Library. Web site: http://www.brown.edu/Facilities/John_Carter_Brown_Library.
13. Library Company of Philadelphia. Web site: http://www.librarycompany.org.
14. Library of Congress Kislak Short-term Fellowship in American Studies. Web site: http://www.loc.gov/loc/kluge/kluge-kislak-short_term.html.
15. Massachusetts Historical Society. Web site: http://www.masshist.org.
16. Monticello. Web site: http://www.monticello.org.
17. Newberry Library. Web site: http://www.newberry.org.
18. New York Academy of Medicine. Web site: http://www.nyam.org.
19. Princeton University Library. Web site: http://library.princeton.edu.
20. Smithsonian American Art Museum. Web site: http://americanart.si.edu.

21. University of Virginia Library. Web site: http://www.lib. virginia.edu
22. Winterthur Museum and Country Estate. Web site: http:// www.winterthur.org.
23. Yale Center for British Art, Yale University. Web site: http:// www.yale.edu/ycba.

Index

Abasi, A.R.; Akbari, N.; and Graves, B. 144

academic integrity: Acadia Institute Graduate Education Project 139-40, 142; authorship issues 145-6; business 150-1; disciplinary distinctions 146-55; education 148-9; and ethics training 156; factors 139-41; gender 140-1; and graduate students 137-67; and honesty colure 156-7; international graduate students 144-5; law 151-2; librarian role 157-61; medicine 154-5; plagiarism 142-5; and plagiarism grading plan 157; prevalence 139-41; psychology 147-8; rationales for dishonesty 141-2; sciences and engineering 152-4; social work 148; sociology 149-50; solutions for graduate dishonesty 155-61; university plagiarism policies 156

Academic Search Premier 175

Acadia Institute; Graduate Education Project 139-40, 142

Ackerson, L.G. 56

advanced information literacy; Germany 70-92

Akbari, N.; Abasi, A.R.; and Graves, B. 144

Altman, E. 157

American Chemical Society (ACS) 53

American Psychological Association 147-8

American Speech-Language-Hearing Association 118, 122

Amodeo, M.; and Collins, M.E. 148

Anderson Computing and Information Services (ACIS) 95, 100-1, 103, 104, 107, 109, 110

Anderson, M.S. 139, 140; *et al* 149-50; Swazey, J.P.; and Louis, K.S. 138-9

Anderson School of Management: eLibrarian virtual reference 98; field study projects 96-8, 106-9; graduate student differences 94-5; InfoIQ competencies 103; InfoIQ and instructional technology and design 109; InfoIQ online delivery 108-9; InfoIQ partner identification 106-7; InfoIQ pilot program 102, 103-6; InfoIQ transition 103; Information Literacy Campaign (ILC) 100-2; just-in-time approach 96-8; Life Cycle of Business Information Needs 100, 101; lifelong information literacy skills 93-111; and MBA information literacy assessment 102-3; MBA life cycle student needs 98, 99; research strategy teaching 96; UCLA 94-111

Ascough, R.S. 21

Associated Canadian Theological Schools: assignments 27-9; course design importance 29-30; course philosophy 25-6; course structure